MW00775980

Life > Limb

MY JOURNEY TO BECOMING WHOLE

John LeMieux

TheBestCo

The author has made every effort to ensure the accuracy of the information within this book was correct at time of publication. The author does not assume and hereby disclaims any liability to any party for any loss, damage, or disruption caused by errors or omissions, whether such errors or omissions result from accident, negligence, or any other cause.

TheBestCo
21 Wildwood Circle
Portland, ME 04103

Copyright © 2021 John LeMieux

Cover design: Karen Richardson

Photographs from family archives

More information at www.johnlemieux.com

ISBN: 978-0-578-87688-7

Library of Congress Control Number: 2021909505

All rights reserved, which includes the right to reproduce this book or portions thereof in any form whatsoever except as provided by the US Copyright Law. For information address John LeMieux.

Contents

Preface 1
Amputation 3
Maine 11
Escape 15
Refuge 19
Scar Tissue 23
Origins 25
The River 27
Ego 31
Tests 35
Maine Central Institute 39
Skip Pound 45
Bodhicitta 49
CaringBridge 53
The Die Is Cast 61
Handicapped 63
Bruce Davis 67
Game On 71
Surgery 77
The Other Side 81
Getting Home 87
Resilience 91
New Year's and New Paradigm 95
Back to Boston 101
Shared History 105
Moments in Time 107

Stoicism	115
Emotional Action	121
Angels and Acceptance	125
Bill Fitzgerald	133
Dependency	139
Cindy	151
Magda Abdou	155
So It Is	159
Coaching	161
Matt Richards	165
Home Work	173
Friends	179
The Dunk That Never Was	185
Building a Leg	193
Adaptation	199
The Day Before I Was Cleared to Walk	203
Closing CaringBridge	209
"Cut the Other One Off and Go Pro"	215
The Last Chapter	221
Author's Note	225
About the Author	229

This book is written the year I will turn sixty-two. My understanding of life, and how I fit into and cope with the vagaries of life, probably began at age four or five. In the interval I have struggled, as we all do, with the pain of living and I have experienced, as we all do, the wonderful gifts that life affords us.

These highs and lows, the roller-coaster of emotional depth that is life must be experienced in tandem. Not one-for-one—a pain for every pleasure—but in concert. For if we don't feel the pleasure, we can't truly understand the pain. And, if the emotional hurt is not real to us, we can't appreciate the wonderful gifts that life does deliver.

This duality of life and its expression in my experience has formed me. But I am not who I am today without the love and understanding of my wife. Cindy Romasco LeMieux, as you will see in my story, is an amazing woman. Her support for me through the loss of my leg and my recovery was encompassing and selfless and heroic. Her efforts on my behalf sustained me physically, emotionally, and mentally through some of the toughest moments one can imagine.

Incredibly, Cindy's effect on my life is far deeper than the support she provided as I struggled with cancer and lost my leg. At a most basic level she modeled the best that the human spirit has to offer. Her empathy and caring for others enlightens everyone who knows her. The years that we were together before my cancer diagnosis were an important antecedent to my ability to begin to understand and deal with my emotions once the loss of my leg became a reality. Her patience and selflessness as I grew into the depth of the man I am today cannot be overstated. There were many times when a lesser person would have run for the hills when faced with the most imperfect and unformed man I was. But she didn't cut and run. She stayed and faced my demons with me—understanding when she could and simply supporting me when she couldn't understand me. Her love made me. Period.

To my love, thank you for being you and daring to be with me. I love you now and for the rest of my life.

Remember this your lifetime through:
Tomorrow there will be more to do.
And failure waits for all who stay
With some success made yesterday.
Tomorrow you must try once more,
And even harder than before.

—John R. Wooden

Basketball Coach UCLA, Ten-time National Champions
Three-time all-American as a player at Purdue University

Preface

Today is the only opportunity to affect tomorrow. I learned that lesson from my high school and college basketball coaches and from studying the philosophy of some of the greatest coaches of the twentieth century. People like John Wooden, who I had the great fortune to meet before his death in 2010.

This I know: We are not promised anything in life, but we get to choose how we respond to what life hands us. When I coached college basketball myself, I told my players that I welcomed mistakes of commission: attempting to do something positive over mistakes of omission: being afraid to attempt something. A coach can correct and teach from something attempted, but it is impossible to correct something that never happened.

When I was told I had cancer I was determined to act. I just didn't know how. I would find out as I went.

Amputation

On December 20, 2012, in an operation that lasted nineteen hours and fifty-six minutes, the doctors at Brigham and Women's Hospital in Boston took off my left leg at the hip socket, separating the bones and cutting away the muscles, tendons, and ligaments that held my hip together. Then in a Frankenstein-type of surgery, they cut through the bone and muscle of that severed leg at a point six inches above my knee, dissected out the nerves that stretched from my torso to the lower leg, rotated my lower leg and knee joint 180 degrees, and attached my shortened thigh bone to my pelvis with eight titanium screws. The vascular surgeons carefully reattached all the major arteries and veins and then the orthopedic surgeons curled up the nerves that had been dissected out and deposited them behind my knee joint into the popliteal space; replaced my surface tissues and closed the wound with 360 degrees of sutures encircling my leg and pelvis. I was left with a shortened left leg with my foot facing backward.

The operation was technically extremely difficult both for the orthopedic surgeon, who took me apart and reconstructed me, and the vascular surgeon who had to reconnect the vital blood vessels to make sure my reattached leg would live. During the almost twenty hours in the operating room, I lost twenty liters of blood and received twenty-six units of packed red blood cells and twenty-six units of fresh frozen plasma, according to the post-operative report. After the operation I was kept sedated for another full day and then very slowly brought to consciousness.

When I awoke, I was in a glass-fishbowl room in the intensive care unit and I saw the bump of my heel, underneath the sheet. That shortened, rotated leg and foot were that all remained of my left leg. I wiggled my toes and flexed my ankle and the sheet moved. The nerves that the doctor had saved worked!

It was then I realized I had a tube down my throat. My wife, Cindy, and sister, Bonnie, were in the brightly lit room full of equipment. I motioned to a pad of paper on the bedside table. My sister handed it to me, and I wrote, "Take the f——ing tube out." I handed her the note and pointed to a gaggle of doctors outside my door. They had the tube out in record time. I tried to orient myself to my new reality. The next six months of my life would be the worst and best I have ever experienced.

Cancer came back. It is that simple. When I was forty-two, I had been diagnosed and successfully treated for sebaceous cell cancer in my right eyelid; what had started as a small bump on my eyelid became a surgeon telling me that I had cancer and there was a 5 percent chance I could die. When he said there was a 5 percent fatality rate I asked if that meant there was a 95 percent opportunity that I would be okay. He said, "Yes." I said, "Let's work with those numbers shall we?" And in the end, following a relatively minor surgery on my right eyelid, I was cancer free.

All was well until ten years later, in May of 2011, when I awoke one morning with the feeling of a charley horse in my left thigh. When I couldn't stretch the stiffness out and a later course of ultrasound therapy failed to break up what I assumed was a calcifying bruise deep in my thigh muscle, I persuaded my family doctor to order an MRI. The MRI (not an easy procedure because of my fear of small spaces—if you have ever had an MRI, you understand) showed a small lesion close to the femur in the vastus intermedius muscle. An ultrasound-guided biopsy showed no cancer, but the consensus among the doctors was that the small, atypical spindle cell lesion should be removed because it didn't belong there and things like that lesion were associated with cancer.

On August 1, 2011, I went in for a two-hour day surgery, four days before my fifty-second birthday. I went into the operating room for a relatively routine procedure—to cut out a cyst—a lesion—a little something that wasn't harmful but should be removed. My wife, Cindy, waited in the hospital during what was a relatively short and straightforward surgery.

When I awoke from the anesthesia Cindy's face was white and she told me the surgeon's first words to her in the waiting room were, "The good news is that we didn't have to take his leg." I could guess the bad news. Even though the earlier biopsy had shown no cancer, the initial lab results of the frozen section and the surgeon's own eyes had told her cancer was there. I was diagnosed with myxofibrosarcoma. It seems strange now, but it took me a couple of days to learn to spell *myxofibrosarcoma*. Today it feels like a word I have known all my life. The second thing the doctor told my wife was that myxofibrosarcoma was called the "cockroach of cancers" because it often reappeared in or near its original location or often in the lungs. Neither was appealing.

"The world breaks everyone and afterward many are strong at the broken places."

—Ernest Hemingway, *A Farewell to Arms.*

During my earlier bout with cancer, I had the opportunity to face my mortality. One morning, before I had the surgery on my eyelid, I was driving through the White Mountains of New Hampshire on my way back to Portland, Maine, from visiting a college friend in the Northeast Kingdom of Vermont. As I drove the winding road on that bright spring day, I realized that cancer might be what kills me. While I didn't hear an audible voice, it might as well have been. I realized quite directly that I would die one day, and that sebaceous cell cancer may be what does it. Intellectually I knew we all die, but at age forty-two my death was supposed to be a distant problem—for me to deal with much later in what I expected to be a long life. Knowing that I might die soon was new. Yet, there was no distress in the thought that the cancer could kill me. I intuitively understood that several billion people had faced death in the history of the world before me and that I would not be alone in discovering the secrets death holds for us all.

Now at age fifty-two, I was faced with the interruption of cancer in my life once again. This time it was not a one-and-done affair. After an eight-week course of localized radiation to attempt to kill the cancer, I ultimately had another three surgeries before the doctors told me the cancer and affected tissue had been cut out. I was sent home in December of 2011 with a gaping wound on my upper thigh that measured eight inches by four inches, shaped roughly like a football and cut deep into my leg. When the wound was cleaned every other day, I could look at my leg and see my iliotibial band and my rectus femoris muscle. My view of my leg was like a real-life picture in an anatomy textbook. It was both bloody and fascinating at once. I couldn't look away. One day when the wound nurse removed the thick bandages that covered the exposed muscle, I felt my leg cramping. I looked into the open wound to see my rectus femoris muscle shuddering and contracting as the cramp enveloped the muscle and the pain registered in my brain.

The surgeon had removed my vastus lateralis and my vastus intermedius as well as scraped the periosteum from my femur in her attempt to make sure the cancer was gone. In the months that followed my wound slowly healed (granulated is the medical term) from the inside out until I was left with a savage but healed scar. The follow-up MRIs and CT scans of my leg, abdomen, and chest came back negative for almost a year. During that time, I built up my strength and endurance, running at least three times a week and completing two 10K road races. Aside from the shark bite–like scar on my leg and the lack of explosive power because the two big muscles had been removed, I was doing quite well, all things considered. I even played a little half-court basketball and some casual tennis.

As I was recovering from these surgeries on my left thigh and strengthening my leg, I wrote the following:

After Cancer
Now what?
The good news is
I am still here
But who am I?
Certainly not like before
Yet still the same

In some ways
Death can be a comfort
The common end for all
But too soon and too fast
Force you to think too much
I'm still me
Weaker, wiser . . . Better?

Weaker in body but stronger in spirit
I know me better now
I know this world better now
I know that life is not about breath
Life is about what you do with that breath
How you live is life

In the end, we are what we do
I am weaker in body
They cut away muscle to save me
I will make my body stronger
Time and toil will see to that
My spirit knows more
And is not satisfied with living as before
It demands exercise too

Maine

In 1963, when I was four, my parents had moved from Brunswick, Maine, where my father grew up, to Hawthorne, California, joining the great exodus of World War II vets with young families looking for good fortune in the bright sun of California. Once in California, with my two-year-old brother, Michael, and my infant sister, Bonnie, my father worked two jobs, bought a house and then a rental property, and strove to save enough money to move back to Maine. My mother, a trained registered nurse, had a full-time job caring for her children and a husband dealing with the ravages of war. Seven hard years later, they felt comfortable enough to drive their station wagon, with four kids now—my brother, Patrick, having been born in 1965—back to Maine.

I was eleven years old when my family moved the 3,000 miles from Los Angeles to Maine. The summer I turned twelve we moved into an old colonial house on eighty acres of land in Bowdoinham, Maine. I think there were more people on my block in Los Angeles than in the whole town of Bowdoinham. The house was a massive gold-and-white, three-story structure with thirteen rooms, a connected two-story barn, a detached barn, and three other outbuildings. It was an old dairy farm with everything you would expect to find on an old farm—including a small family cemetery on a low hill a hundred yards behind the house overlooking a bubbling brook that meandered through the fields on the edge of the woods. In the woods were old Ford Model-Ts and collections of bottles and cans that were the remnants of all the families that had farmed the land in the 150 years the farm had been there.

The house sat on Main Street and had a circular dirt driveway that went completely around the house anchored by two great oak trees on the front lawn. It had a formal front entrance that led to a grand staircase in the front hall, a side door that we used each day on the left side of the house, and a door that opened off the laundry room on the right side at the back of the house.

The laundry room door—with its small porch—overlooked my first basketball court, although court is too generous a description. It consisted of a hard-packed piece of dirt about thirty feet wide and twenty-five feet deep. Our backboard was a piece of half-inch plywood, painted white with a faded red square, suspended by a hodgepodge of two-by-fours nailed to an ancient light pole. An ancient light fixture, that had provided light since electricity first came to the farm, lit the hoop. The rusty rim was approximately ten feet off the ground. When it was dry you could almost dribble on the lumpy, packed ground. When it rained it was mud. We played in the sun, the rain, and the snow.

In many ways it was like any number of other baskets that kids learned to shoot at all over America. It did have one defining characteristic: years earlier a large chestnut tree had been cut down when the roots began to affect the light pole and the tree's stump—three feet high and fifteen inches across—still remained just four feet to the right side of the backboard. That stump was the launching point for my first dunk. Basketball was never the same for me after that experience and basketball became a central part of my life for the next twenty-two years as a player and a coach.

Much of who I am and how I navigate the world began on that patch of hardened mud on Main Street and on the buckled asphalt court that spanned the width of a tennis court behind the Bowdoinham Community School. Whether I was shooting at our hoop with my brothers until my mother called us in for the night or playing pickup games behind the school where the chain-link fence was inbounds if your body hit it but out-of-bounds if a ball bounced off it, basketball became my home away from home—my escape from the times when life intruded rudely on my boyhood world. The lessons that basketball taught me over the decades had their genesis in those moments in that small town. How I handled cancer and amputation started there.

Escape

I initially played basketball as an escape—an escape from the world my father created. He came back from his service as a marine in World War II a tormented man. He wasn't inherently bad. He could laugh and have fun, but he was anxious and angry and he wore his emotions on his sleeve. By the time I was born in 1959 when he was thirty-four years old, he had been married and divorced twice and had two other children that he rarely saw.

He and my mother were married in 1957. As an adult I found out that they got married in a civil ceremony after my mother had become pregnant and because the Catholic Church wouldn't let a divorced man marry in the church. Before they were married that spring, they gave my older sister up for adoption and then after they were married, they attempted to get her back from a Catholic agency that refused to return her. That loss only increased my father's pain and scarred my mother for life. I never knew my sister existed until I was in my late thirties. The wound was so deep my parents never discussed her. I knew of my half sisters from my father's first two marriages, but never of my older sister.

This pattern of shame and secrecy was to be repeated over and over in my parents' lives and ultimately came to affect my brothers and sister and me in very difficult ways. My father was quick to anger and my mother was resigned to life without her firstborn. They both lacked an ability to act reasonably in the face of the normal daily stress of raising four children in the sixties and seventies.

My father's demanding nature caused me to fear his presence. I would literally quiver when I heard the crunch of his car tires in the driveway. My mind would race as I tried to determine if I had left any chore undone or done a half-assed job on an assigned task. As the oldest child, the others were my responsibility and if their work was undone or shoddy, it could be my fault. I was afraid most of the time.

When my father found something that was not done or not done to his satisfaction, he took extreme measures. One night when I was twelve or thirteen, he found a pan that I had washed that wasn't as clean as he wanted. His response was to have me scrub every pot, pan, cookie sheet, and griddle in our kitchen. He demanded years of cooked-on blackness be removed. I was in the kitchen until midnight with my hands literally raw from the steel wool and abrasive soap as I returned every vessel to its original, pristine state. To this day I wash dishes very thoroughly.

Another favorite tactic of my father's was what today are called "stress positions" by the CIA. If we failed at some tasks, we could be made to kneel on a wood floor in the corner of a room facing the wall for thirty minutes or more.

After five or ten minutes the kneecaps on both legs would go numb and then five minutes later, they would begin to hurt, ache, and then burn with pain. I can remember kneeling in the front formal living room away from the rest of the family while the sun went down. As it got dark outside, I was afraid I had been forgotten but more afraid to move. Eventually my father hollered that I could get up.

While my father was not physically violent too often, he made up for the infrequency with his intensity. Once when we were living in Los Angeles and my brother Michael was seven, he ran away from home prompting a search by the neighbors and eventually the police. When I finally found him on Manhattan Beach, three miles from home, five or six hours later, he was sent to his room to await my father. When my father got home instead of going into the room, picking up his son and telling him how much he loved him and how scared he had been, my father beat him. He used a two-by-one slat from a bunk bed, a plastic bowling pin, and a leather belt to try and make sure his son would stay and never leave home again. As I had been the one to find my brother, I felt that his beating was my fault. It was just one more part of my life that was out of my control. Even if I had placed myself between my father and my brother, I couldn't have stopped the beating he received and at age nine I think I knew that was the truth.

Refuge

Basketball became my refuge. I started playing on my junior high team in the seventh grade when I was twelve. We practiced in the Bowdoinham Town Hall as our school didn't have a gymnasium. The old building had served the town for more than one hundred years when I first entered its doors. It was a simple, functional space designed for town meetings and contra dances. The tall, double, heavy wooden doors opened into the space across a narrow hall and a set of smaller interior doors. The maple floor was old and slippery and hadn't seen a coat of polyurethane in decades. A stage rose four feet above the floor at the end of the hall opposite the main doors. Downstairs there were restrooms, storerooms, and an ancient kitchen. In the back behind the stage, the town fathers had office space.

The hall itself was only about fifty feet across. Our court ran sideways across the room, parallel to the stage and the doors that opened to the street outside. In the winter the wind could blow snow into the room if both sets of doors stayed open too long.

The two baskets were mounted almost flush on the walls between windows that stretched twenty feet high and were covered with chicken wire to protect them from our flying basketballs. We learned that we could dribble toward the wall, jump, and then push off the wall with our foot to dunk the ball. We also learned how hard those walls could be if you slipped and stumbled into them. The old chandelier that lit the room was suspended from the ceiling thirty feet above us. The hall was heated by a single cast-iron radiator and when the sun went down the room felt immediately colder—like stepping into the shadows on a winter's day. We often started practice in sweatpants or with long johns underneath our basketball shorts until our body heat and activity warmed the room. I wasn't particularly good at first, but I loved to play and my time on my homemade court and behind the community school paid off and I was a starter in the eighth grade.

When I was on the court there were rules—and referees who impartially enforced those rules. It was a safe place for me. I was rewarded for good effort and I had chances to make up for mistakes with the next play or, at worst, the next game. In the eighth grade we got a new coach. Lance Libby was a young teacher who immediately recognized that his group had some talent and that we were hungry to play. After we finished our twelve- or fourteen-game junior high schedule, he called up other coaches and drove us all over southern Maine to play. That winter I wore out my sneakers and told my father I wanted a pair of the cool black-and-white Converse All Stars high tops I saw the pros wear on the ABC *NBA Game of the Week*. He thought the Converse were too expensive and bought me a generic pair of sneakers. I wore them so often and played so hard I had holes in the bottoms that I covered with cardboard insoles until I could convince him to get me a new pair. Of the five starters on that junior high team three of us played and started for our regional high school. I was the only one that would go on to play varsity basketball in college.

Although my school teammates liked basketball, I lived and breathed it. I didn't need anyone else to be on the court to shoot and play my fantasy games. I was Jerry West or Connie Hawkins or John Havlicek or the best of all three rolled into one. I dribbled and twisted and shot the game-winning shot a hundred times a day; and whenever I missed, it was because I was fouled. But I had the chance to make it right by trying again or by making two foul shots. When I would miss my free throws in my make-believe games, I created a lane violation on an imaginary defender to give me the second chance I needed. After that eighth-grade season, I went to the community school court every day in the spring, summer, and early fall, often from morning to evening. I would bring a sandwich for lunch and go into the cemetery across the street from the school to sit in the shade. After a half hour I would fill my gallon jug with water from the hose and then go back into the sun and begin again.

Eventually, I developed written practice routines to make sure I was working on skills that would translate to the actual games I loved. I had a forty-five-minute workout that I would do with different drills: shooting, dribbling, defensive slides, and throwing a ball off the backboard as high as I could to practice snatching a rebound. I did these drills at different speeds with more intense activities followed by foul shots so I could rest. I also developed a six-hour morning and afternoon workout that I would break up with my lunch break. That workout involved all my drills but also running and sprinting to make sure I was always in better shape than anyone else. If I failed at a drill, I would make myself run a sprint up and back the length of the tennis court. I learned to run backward almost as fast as I could forward with the idea that I could backpedal down the court and still see all the other players. These were solitary workouts. If someone came along, I would challenge them to games of one-on-one and occasionally we would have enough players to play four-on-four on our short court surrounded by chain link. In the summer when the older guys would come home from college, I improved more quickly facing their better size, strength, and speed—even if they weren't good basketball players. But mostly it was me and a ball, the asphalt, the sun, the rim, and the chain-link fence. I was safe and I was rewarded for my efforts as I got better.

Scar Tissue

I spent the spring and summer of 2012 strengthening my leg after all the surgeries had cut the cancer from my body, and running with my friend, Bruce Davis, as we trained for the L.L.Bean 10K in July and another 10K in August. Bruce and I had met when he and my wife were in graduate school studying for their masters degrees in social work. When Bruce heard I was training for the 10K he asked if he could join my training runs. He did and we met Mondays, Wednesdays, and Fridays at 6:30 a.m. to run.

In the early fall of 2012, after a five-mile run during a vacation on Martha's Vineyard I felt a tightness in my upper left thigh. When I reported the tightness to my oncologist and my general practitioner both doctors thought that because of my continued exercise regimen, I might be growing muscle tissue into the three-inch-wide and seven-inch-long surgical scar that remained deep in my thigh. They thought the muscle tissue was being trapped and pinched by the scars and that was the pain I felt.

We decided on a dual course of action: physical therapy to break up the scar tissue and a new MRI to see what the tightness looked like to a radiologist. While I waited for the MRI, I did what I always had done and dove into physical therapy. The physical therapist manipulated the scar bed and I worked diligently to stretch and improve my range of motion. I thought if I worked my body hard enough, I could beat back whatever was happening. The cancer had been cut out of my leg. I had the scars to prove it. It was up to me to make myself better.

While the initial physical therapy results were encouraging no one was surprised when the MRI results indicated the strong likelihood of a recurrent tumor.

When I had originally been diagnosed with myxofibrosarcoma, I had made the two-hour drive to Boston and met with an oncologist at the Dana Farber Cancer Center, a hospital acknowledged as one of the best cancer centers in the world. With my new MRI in hand, I went for a return visit.

At Dana Farber, my oncologist reviewed the MRI and said things didn't look good. The previous surgeries had cut away much of the muscle tissue of my thigh and the new tumor had now infiltrated what was left. He had asked a surgeon to review the MRI and when he joined our meeting, he confirmed the oncologist's diagnosis: if this were the cancer it appeared to be, it would be impossible to perform another operation to cut out the cancer and leave me with a functioning leg.

The surgeon, Dr. Marco Ferrone, did have a potential solution. I was not ready for what I was about to hear.

Origins

In 1927 in Europe, Dr. J. Borggreve first performed a surgery that replaced the weakened knee of a twelve-year-old boy suffering from tuberculosis by making amputation cuts across the tibia and the fibula below the knee and across the femur above the knee. The knee joint itself was replaced by attaching the tibia—rotated 180 degrees—to the femur with plates and screws. The nerves that provided feeling to the lower leg were dissected out and kept intact. The blood vessels were cut and reattached. The result was a foot and ankle, facing backwards, that allowed a prosthetic leg to be attached and the child to return home with the prospect of good ambulatory ability. Rather than suffer an amputation leaving no limb below mid-thigh, the patient was able to use the backward-facing ankle as a knee joint. Dr. Borggreve published reports of his surgical technique in 1930 and rotationplasty became a rare but effective solution to treat severe infections and tumors of the knee joint that would have previously resulted in amputation mid-thigh. In 1950, Dutch orthopedist, Cornelis Pieter van Nes, published results of rotationplasty surgeries he was performing and he became the surgeon most well-known for rotationplasties. The surgeries were most often performed on children.

Later, Dr. Winfried Winkelmann, a German, began to do rotationplasty surgeries that replaced the hip of the patient with the knee joint to prevent hip disarticulation amputations from cancerous tumors high up in the thigh. By taking the distal femur and the knee joint intact, rotating them 180 degrees, and reattaching them to the pelvis of his patient he allowed rotationplasty to benefit a whole new class of patients. His "B–1" variation on the Van Nes rotationplasty technique was the surgery used to cut out my cancer, save my life, and provide me with the chance to have a functional prosthetic.

The River

My experience has led me to the understanding that life is relentless. It just keeps going no matter what we do. When I was in my early teens, we used to jump from the upstream side of the Route 24 bridge over the Cathance River in Bowdoinham. When we hit the water, no matter how strong a swimmer we were or how hard we pulled, we were swiftly taken downstream. The river's current was relentless. We could keep our head above water and eventually make it to shore, but we were always further downstream from where we began.

Now, as I faced the return of this "cockroach of cancers," I realized again that life's current was in control. Just as when I jumped from the bridge and had learned to judge the current and how hard I had to swim to reach shore, at age fifty-three I was learning to swim in a powerful current again.

Understanding that life is relentless is not the same as surrendering to the idea that fate is in control, that we have no say in our outcomes. Had I allowed the current to take me when I dove off my bridge I would have eventually floated down the river to Merrymeeting Bay and then out into the wide Atlantic Ocean. But I didn't just float downstream. I managed the current and swam to shore. As I faced the reoccurrence of myxofibrosarcoma in my thigh, I began to pull a little harder to make my way to shore.

Dr. Ferrone said I was faced with two choices: an amputation of my leg at the hip (a hip-disarticulation) with no real chance of a workable prosthetic, or an extremely complicated and dangerous surgery that had never been attempted on a person my age. According to the doctor, the second option would—after hours in the operating room and months of rehab—leave me with the equivalent of a functional below-the-knee amputation with an expectation that I could jog again and play golf on my new artificial leg. According to the surgeon this unique surgery would involve removing my leg at the hip, scarfing my existing hip joint to remove the ball-and-socket joint that had held my leg in place at the hip, cutting away the cancer-infected upper thigh, making another cut through my leg bone above my knee, and reattaching my healthy knee and ankle at the hip. But there was a catch. To have the most function in my repaired leg, the knee and ankle would have to be rotated 180 degrees before they were reattached, leaving me with a shortened leg facing backward—my knee joint functioning as a hip and my ankle joint, with its backward facing foot, taking the place of my knee. A prosthetic would attach to my lower leg, ankle, and foot to reach to the ground and allow me to walk.

For a moment as the surgeon described this rotationplasty surgery my mind raced ahead to how I would look with one normal leg and the other a shortened, backward facing foot, hanging about fifteen inches from the ground. My stomach got very tight. As the doctor finished his description of the surgery, he made the statement that made all the difference. He said that if the cancer had not spread to my lungs or abdomen and the surgery was successful, I could be cured of cancer. I began to swim toward shore.

Ego

As a child when I got in trouble my father often made me go to his closet and get his thick leather belt that he would use to spank me. That walk up the stairs and back down again with that heavy belt in my small hands was brutal and filled with the expectation of the pain to come. As I got older (after age thirteen or so) the spankings stopped but he could still stand me straight up with an open hand slap and lift me off the ground by my collar. Eventually I got big enough that I could have stood my ground and inflicted my own pain had I dared. But I didn't. I couldn't. I was too afraid.

I had grown to be six foot two inches and 170 pounds but the me that people on the outside saw didn't reflect the scared young man that lived inside me. My relationship with my father had caused me to doubt who I was and to second-guess myself in almost every situation. Basketball was one of the few areas of my life, along with singing in a school choir group, where I had anything that resembled confidence.

When I was a senior in high school I began to be recruited by some small colleges in New England. I was good enough that the college coaches thought I could be helpful, but I was not on anyone's radar as a player who would make an impact. Because I had worked so hard on my game, I had leapfrogged many of the players in my school. I went from a part-time player as a junior to a starter as a senior. In the first game of my senior year, playing Oxford Hills High School in a small town in the western Maine mountains, I was the leading scorer in the victory. Several times in the fall of my senior year I led our team in scoring and everyone knew I was always in fantastic shape because in addition to our high school practices, I ran for miles and lifted weights with my legs several times a week.

As part of the recruiting process, I received an essay from a college coach that outlined the qualities of a "winner." I showed the essay to my high school coach as I did almost everything I got from a college. The next day my coach gave me a three-page handwritten letter. In the letter he took me to task in no uncertain terms about my ego and inflated sense of myself as a ballplayer. One line from that letter rang through the missive like a bell. He wrote, "If I can accomplish one thing—to make you realize that your head band is too tight—then I will be successful." In other words, my ego was too big. We started to talk after I read his letter and that coach, Nelson Beaudoin, changed the course of my life.

My high school, Mt. Ararat, was a brand-new school. Not just a new school building but a brand-new entity. After decades of the children from Bowdoin, Bowdoinham, Topsham, and Harpswell going to Brunswick High School, a new school district was formed and the new high school built. My freshman year was the first year of operation. Nelson was the young coach tasked with building a varsity basketball program from scratch. In his first two years he didn't have much success with converted football players and good athletes who tried basketball for fun. By my junior year Nelson had built the nucleus for the team that would go 12–8 my senior year. He ran after-school clinics and took us to summer camps, and we played in off-season leagues as we strived to get better as individuals and as a team. He had put in the time to make us better as players and his effort with me was a continuation of that process.

After many, many talks I realized that coaches could help people and I knew then that I wanted to coach too. Nelson and his wife helped me immeasurably through some very difficult times and from the age of seventeen, until I was thirty-four, very nearly everything I did was prefaced by the question, "Will this make me a better college basketball coach?" My college choices, summer jobs, graduate school . . . all were predicated on whether they would help me as a coach. I set a goal to be a head college basketball coach by the time I was thirty. I became a head coach at age twenty-eight. The same focus I used to accomplish that goal would be applied in many other areas of my life. It all started with Nelson's caring.

Tests

Before we could consider the surgery we needed to make sure the cancer had not spread. If it turned out that the cancer had spread, not only would I not be a candidate for the complicated rotationplasty surgery, but I could be facing the reality of death in a matter of weeks, months, or years depending on how invasive the spreading cancer had become.

A positron emission tomography (PET) scan was ordered. PET scans are usually painless with the exception of the injection used to introduce the radioactive materials called radiopharmaceuticals or radiotracers that help doctors see if cancer has spread. The most used radiotracer is F–18 fluoro-deoxyglucose—or FDG. In many ways it is like sugar water with radioactive material mixed in. Because cancer cells are more metabolically active, they may absorb glucose (sugar) at a higher rate that can be seen on PET scans. This allows your doctor to identify disease before it may be seen on other imaging tests. The radiotracers show up in the cancerous areas as bright images within the body. The doctors say the areas "light up." Think of a view of the United States at night from outer space. The bright, well-lit areas along the east and west coasts and big cities in the Midwest would be the cancer, while the darker interior parts of the country are the healthy tissues.

In addition to the PET scan, I would need a biopsy of the tumor to make sure the mass we could see on the MRI was in fact the type of cancer everyone expected it to be. It was a formality that needed to be completed as a precursor to the surgery.

The PET scan was scheduled within five days of my appointment at Dana Farber. My oncologist in Portland worked hard to get me scheduled quickly. The biopsy would be a week after the PET scan.

When I went into the special isolation area where they inject you with the radioactive solution for the PET scan—in the customized trailer outside the main building of the cancer center—I was struck by how high tech this all was. After I received my injection, I had to sit quietly in a darkened room while the material spread throughout my body. The waiting was made tougher by the slowly developing feeling of warmth that overtook me and the beginnings of the need to urinate. After forty-five minutes I was marinated enough for them to take me to the other end of the capsule and lay me on a cold, hard slab for my scan. The scan itself was over in just a few minutes and I was on my way to the restroom.

As Cindy and I waited for the PET scan and its thumbs-up or thumbs-down indication of the direction my life would take, we discussed the duality in front of us. If my lungs lit up like Manhattan on a clear night, we would be faced with my death from cancer, and it would be just a matter of time.

Cindy and I had been married for fifteen years and we had lived through the loss of my father and both her parents as well as her brother. Cindy wasn't ready to lose her husband too. It was a difficult time full of unknowns and dark possibilities.

Privately, I began to think of the concept of "dying well." I realized that death was certainly not new to the human condition, but I still wondered how I would deal with death when death as a concept became my reality. I reviewed my estate documents and talked with my business partner about our continuity plans.

The other outcome would be that the PET scan showed that the cancer was only in my thigh. That would be the good news. The good news would allow them to cut off my leg!

As I swam in the current of the relentless river of my life, I realized that I needed to reframe the concept of losing my leg. If they could do the surgery that would take my leg it would mean that I would have a very high expectation that I would be cured of cancer. Cured. At age fifty-three that could mean another twenty-five or thirty years of life.

After the PET scan was complete and I got the call that the results were in, I returned to see my oncologist. I came to the appointment by myself—I wanted to have mental and emotional space if the news was bad before I faced my wife and my family.

When the doctor walked into the small, brightly lit

examination room he smiled. There was good news. The PET scan showed that the cancer had not spread! "Good," I said, "now they can cut off my leg." I said it with a smile because it was good news. I did not have cancer invading the rest of my body. It was trapped in my thigh and we could get it!

As I contemplated the surgery and later made my way through the pain, emotions, and struggle that followed the removal and reattachment of my leg, I drew strength from the simple equation: **Life > Limb**. Life is greater than limb. It is true.

Maine Central Institute

In the early spring of my senior year in high school I had decided to play basketball at Gordon College in Wenham, Massachusetts. After my senior season I had made the ninety-minute drive for an overnight recruiting visit to meet the coaching staff and the players and tour this small, very Christian college. After dinner on that night the players took me into Boston to see the film *Uptown Saturday Night.* I was the only white guy in the theater. I looked forward to playing in greater Boston and the new life experiences I could see in front of me. However, I never played at Gordon. In May of my senior year, I received my financial aid letter and the promised aid had not materialized. I decided instead to spend the next winter at Maine Central Institute in Pittsfield, Maine.

MCI had an outstanding reputation as a post-graduate school where football and basketball players would spend a year after high school to get better or stronger or improve their grades, or in some instances, all three. In addition to the post-graduates there were high school–age boarding students from around the country and around the world as well as local students from three surrounding towns in central Maine. Over the years many basketball players had gone from MCI to major college programs all over the country and I planned to join those ranks. My grades were mediocre in high school from a combination of my poor self-worth and my incongruent but heightened sense that basketball would get me through. However, I had been admitted to several colleges, so I didn't see the need to focus on schoolwork. I went to MCI to get better and stronger. I would soon learn how difficult that would be.

When I walked into my dorm room in Mansion Hall my roommate was already there, lying on his bed on the right side of the room reading. At six foot two he was skinny and as long the bed and had a mop of red hair. At the foot of his bed were three liquor boxes filled with books. Both of Mike Whaley's parents were English teachers and he loved to read as much as I did. We would read those eighty or ninety books before Christmas. During Christmas break we went to his parents' house in Durham, New Hampshire, and brought another three boxes of books back for the spring semester. That fall, my days consisted of a workout before breakfast, classes, lunch, a pickup game with my new teammates in the gym, dinner, study hours in our room, and then reading up to and after lights out. My friendship with Mike has spanned more than forty years at this writing.

Mike was a gifted athlete. I was known as a quick player who could jump and who played harder than anyone else. Mike was a full step quicker than I was and while I played basketball as a mission to redeem myself, he played for the joy of the game. I would never be the athlete he was. Our next-door neighbors in the dorm were Nelson Gosline, a six-foot-four forward I competed against when he played at our rival, Gardiner High School, and Randy Kinzley, who was Mike's teammate at Oyster River High School in Durham, New Hampshire. Randy was as driven as I was—even more so— while Nelson was mostly thinking about his girlfriend back home.

Randy was the first person I had ever met who even came close to working out as hard as I did. If I went for an early morning run in a windbreaker with sand-filled pockets serving as my poor man's weight vest, I often came back to campus just after sunrise to see Randy returning from his own run, or more likely, a trip to the bare-bones weight room in the basement of our gymnasium. Randy also exposed me to my first "it's you or me mentality." Even though he was a better player than me, we were both seen as guards and he didn't plan on me stealing any playing time from him. In truth, I was really a small forward who didn't have his shot or ball-handling skills (he went on to be the starting point guard at the University of New Hampshire) but he was taking no chances. He beat me on the court every chance he could.

Randy's focus on playing time was real because one of our teammates was the best point guard in the eastern US—if not the nation. Dwan Chandler was being recruited by every college I had ever heard of. If we went to pick up our mail together, I might get a letter from my brother, Michael, and a piece of mail from a small college coach or two. Dwan came back to the dorm with a box of letters and shiny brochures from schools like Iowa or North Carolina or Kentucky. Boxes of letters every week. Hundreds of them. Dwan ended up being the starting point guard on some very good Boston College teams in the late seventies and early eighties.

Randy's real threat for playing time came from my roommate and his old high school teammate. As quick and talented as Dwan was (and he was very quick and extremely talented) he had a difficult time getting around Mike Whaley. Mike was lightening quick with both lateral and vertical quickness. He also had a jump shot he could get off on anybody. Mike would dribble at you, make a little shimmy to freeze you, rise up, and release his shot before you even recognized what he was doing. Quickness personified.

Unfortunately, Mike Whaley was directly involved in helping to teach me that life wasn't fair in any shape, form, or fashion. Late in the fall of our year at MCI, before the season really got started, Mike tore his ACL and spent the fall and all of January in a cast from his hip to his ankle following surgery to repair his knee ligament. By the time the cast came off, our season was almost over and he could only watch as we wrapped things up. Eventually Mike rehabbed his knee and went to the University of Bridgeport before leaving there to play at Lyndon State College in Vermont.

The other lesson that came out of my time at MCI had to do with the difference between effort and work. I learned this lesson from three people: Frank Haseltine, who taught science; David Mosher who taught math; and Harry "Pinky" True, the headmaster of MCI. Haseltine and Mosher wouldn't accept the fact that I had already been accepted to college and therefore, in my mind, didn't need to pay attention to my classes. No, if I was in their class then I was going to perform. It wasn't enough to put in effort on something. Effort was important but work produced an output, a result. There was something to show for your effort: a good grade on a test or a paper; a jump shot that was more consistent; or even simply the ability to be consistent in your effort. It was at MCI that I really began to realize that focused hard work could be its own reward.

Harry True, who became a lifelong friend, was responsible for me being at MCI. He allowed my father to pay a little bit each week to cover my tuition and for me to work at odd jobs around campus to pay off what my father couldn't provide. In addition, Harry, who had received the nickname "Pinky" when he was a five-foot-four-inch point guard for the University of Southern Maine, stepped in to help our basketball team when it became apparent that our coach, who was a very nice English teacher from New York, couldn't handle the strong personalities we all brought to the gym. Harry knew basketball and he knew young men. As small as he was, he had no problem backing a six-foot-seven or six-foot-eight young man into a corner if he needed to as he made his points. He expected us to perform on the court and in the classroom and to comport ourselves as nice young men around town. As time went on, I came to appreciate Harry more and more.

Skip Pound

After MCI, I attended Castleton State College in Castleton, Vermont, for a semester. They had recruited me aggressively and I loved the campus, the area, and Lake Bomoseen, where on hot fall afternoons we could have a cold beer at the Dog, the college bar at the Lake Bomossen Inn that had grown famous decades earlier for a dog that would sip beer while sitting on a barstool. While I was getting a lot of playing time as a freshman, the coach who had recruited me was not a good Xs and Os coach and I did not think he was going to help me in my goal to become a college coach.

I left in January to transfer to Concord College in Athens, West Virginia, which had been my second-choice school. I was ineligible because I had transferred but worked out hard to get ready for my sophomore season. In the meantime, Castleton had hired a new coach and my girlfriend and my friends were there so I transferred back for the fall. Unfortunately, I was ineligible for the fall semester because of transferring. Again.

The new young coach at Castleton was talented and eventually, years later when we both coaching, we became friends but my time at Castleton was not fulfilling. The day I met the new coach he was twenty-four and I was twenty. We played a game of H-O-R-S-E and I had him at H-O-R-S. I decided to win the game by making a shot I knew he couldn't physically do. I showed off. I bounced the ball on the floor, it flew high above the rim and I jumped, turned 180 degrees, caught the ball, and dunked it behind my head. He may have been impressed by the dunk, but he was not impressed by me. My time playing for Castleton would prove to be short-lived.

By the time I was a junior in college I was playing for another person who would change the way I saw the world. Darrell "Skip" Pound had returned from a stint as a US Marine Corps officer in Vietnam to serve as the athletic director and basketball coach at Lyndon State College in the Northeast Kingdom of Vermont. I first met Skip during my sophomore year when Castleton State and Lyndon State played at Castleton. Mike Whaley was playing at Lyndon and he and I were chatting after the game when Skip came up. Mike said something smart to Skip and Skip said, "Just because you had a good game don't think you're on my good side." I looked at Skip and asked, "What does it take to get on a coach's good side?" He winked and said, "Transfer to Lyndon." Eventually I did.

Skip had a unique, direct way of working with his players. He treated us like the young men we were and expected us to perform in all the important areas of life. Basketball (or later baseball and soccer—he coached them all) was simply his entrée into our lives. Through the basketball we played, often against teams with superior athletic ability, I learned how to accept what was and use the time I had to address the things I might be able to change. While we were often undersized versus our opponents, we never thought we were beat before the ball was tossed up to begin the game and we won just enough games that others knew not to take us for granted. In my junior year, we qualified for the Mayflower Conference Tournament, exceeding the expectations of the coaches in our league and Skip and even surprising ourselves.

I started both years I played for Skip and was a team captain my senior year, but my real contribution to our team was in my work ethic. I was always working hard and if someone let up in practice, I would embarrass them by grabbing a rebound away or making a steal or driving past them for a bucket. Or I would call them out and demand they keep up with me. I only knew one way to play . . . all out. I was always in shape. I ran on the college cross country team (as their number two or three runner) just to get in shape for hoops. I thought nothing of ten-mile training runs. Once I met a girl at a dance and we agreed to meet the next morning at her house for breakfast, I put my clothes in a backpack and ran the eight miles to her house. I used to tell Skip that if he ever designed a practice that would hurt me, he would kill the other guys. The other thing I could do was jump. I had worked for years to build explosive power in my legs. My vertical leap was thirty-nine-and-a-half inches and everyone we played knew they had to be aware of where I was on the court. I was a one-footed leaper and jumped best off my left leg. More than once I hit the rim with the back of my head when dunking backwards.

While basketball was critically important to me and became my livelihood for eight years, I was not a great basketball player. I played small college basketball and had some success at the regional level, but I was never an all-American or even close. After college I spoke with some people about going to Ireland to play professionally but before I could go the entire league folded. That said, I was a very dedicated basketball player. Skip took my desire and drive and taught me when it was time to work and when it was time to play and to dedicate myself to whatever was at hand. He taught me to leave everything on the court and be satisfied with the outcome—lessons I use to this day.

Bodhicitta

A strange thing happened to me as I began to deal with my original myxofibrosarcoma diagnosis. I began to think like a Buddhist. I didn't know it at the time—I really hadn't studied Buddhism at all—but I was developing "bodhicitta" or enlightened attitude. I was able to see my situation as a part of a larger human condition much as I had come to some understanding about death before my sebaceous cell cancer surgery ten years earlier. I knew, inherently, that while I had to face my own journey within my own diagnosis, I was not alone. Many, many others have walked my walk before me.

It wasn't just those with a cancer diagnosis that understood my reality and that knowledge gave me peace in what should have been a time of deep turmoil. My journey was the shared path of all who have had their life upended without notice or warning. All of us have felt the irreversible hand of life either gently guide or firmly push us in the direction our life was to go. My diagnosis was no different than any other life-threatening diagnosis. It was also no different than the rending emotions of a parent with a child dying too young, the seemingly unnecessary suffering of an aging, dying parent, or the tortures of a soldier coming home from war. It was the shared experience that we are not in control. The experiences we all must confront at some point in our lives.

In November of 2012, before we had a date for the surgery I wrote:

> I am not very good at identifying emotions in the best of times. I once asked a friend who was a therapist to send me a page listing the various emotions because I really have a hard time listing much more than happy, sad, or angry.
>
> As I face the surgery that will cure me of cancer but result at the very least, in a prosthetic below my knee and at worst, the loss of my leg at the hip, I am strangely calm. I don't think I am tamping down emotions because I do get sad at the loss of my leg but, at the same time, I know the operation will cut out the cancer that threatens to kill me decades before I reach old age.
>
> I am sometimes scared about what the rehab will entail, both the physical and the emotional effort it will take to move me forward. I am concerned about how people will see me as I either walk down the street with the new prosthetic leg or make my way with two crutches and one leg. I am vain enough to worry about how I will be seen by others while

at the same time I have gained a much deeper awareness and appreciation for those with physical differences that I see on the street or throughout my day. Whereas before I might have seen a young man with a limp and not have paid much attention, now I look to see what is causing his limp and how he is coping with steps or curbs or slippery sidewalks. He is me in a couple of months.

How will I cope? Will my attitude stay positive or will I slowly become a bitter and angry person? I think I know the answers but until I ultimately face the questions how will I know?

More than anything else I want to protect Cindy in all of this. I know she will hurt emotionally as I hurt physically and if my emotions are too deep and too painful, she will feel them almost as though she were me. Right now, I am focused on the next thing. I hope I am as good when the future becomes the present.

CaringBridge

As Cindy, my family, and our friends began to comprehend the enormity of the potential surgery I had started using the internet-based CaringBridge site so we could keep our family and friends updated on any news without having to call or email everyone independently. These entries allowed me (and occasionally Cindy) to share with everyone what we were experiencing in almost real time. When we set up the CaringBridge site I saw it as an expedient way to process information. It turned out to be a lifeline for me as I recovered from the surgery.

Because the surgeons were planning to reattach my lower leg to my femur using titanium screws, they explained that I would be immobile for a period of time until the femur and my pelvis fused into one bone. When I first heard this, I assumed it meant no weight-bearing on my leg until it healed—like a broken leg. What I did not know, but soon would become apparent was that this was not like a broken leg in any way, shape, form, or fashion. The years following my surgery would be transformative for me and much harder on my family than any of us anticipated.

CaringBridge Post
November 19, 2012
Bone scan results at MCCM
31 days before the surgery

I met with my oncologist at Maine Center for Cancer Medicine (MCCM) this morning to go over the results of my recent bone scan. The scan showed no cancer in my bones other than immediately near the tumor in my upper thigh. In his opinion this shouldn't prevent the doctors at Dana Farber from using the Modified Van Nes rotationplasty surgery that they had previously suggested. I meet with my oncologist and surgeon at Dana Farber on November 28. In the end it will be their call. I am feeling good about the potential to have a functional below-the-knee prosthetic versus an amputation at the hip.

Overall, I feel good. My leg is not overly painful, and I am able to keep ahead of the pain with over-the-counter medication. I am still walking several times a week and am redoubling my efforts around a good diet—just in time for Thanksgiving!

Thanks to everyone for all the kind words, good wishes, and prayers.

It was after this post that my friends and even people I did not know well started to respond on the CaringBridge site. One of my former players who had only played one season for me before I left coaching, Matt Godbout, at that time an executive with an NFL team, wrote back, ". . . we're made to persist, that's how we find out who we are." He couldn't have known how prophetic his words would be.

In the meantime, Cindy and I and a growing army of friends were rehabbing the first-floor apartment in the two-family home we owned to allow me to live there when I returned from the surgery. We had friends show up to do a tremendous amount of work—work that I could no longer do because of the pain and immobility in my leg.

As time went on and the tumor in my upper left thigh continued to grow, it became increasingly difficult to do any meaningful work. I could hardly walk and certainly couldn't sand or paint or clean. Our good friend Steve Jordan, a master electrician in his younger days, completely rewired the apartment after we moved walls to enlarge a bedroom and reconfigured the bathroom to make it handicap accessible. After the construction work was done, we had two or three ten- to twelve-hour days with our friends hard at work to make everything ready for me.

CaringBridge Post
November 25, 2012
Thanks for the help today
26 days before the surgery

Thanks to John and Caroline, Truc, Mike, Willie, Steve and Bruce and Alice. Because of all your hard work Cindy and I made great strides in getting the first-floor apartment ready . . .

I go to Dana Farber on Wednesday 11-28 to meet with the doctors and see what they will suggest re: which surgery to do . . .

CaringBridge Post
November 28, 2012
Recent news
23 days before the surgery

There is much to report. Dana Farber rescheduled my meetings that were originally scheduled for today until next Friday (12-7) so I can meet with the orthopedic surgeon, the vascular surgeon, the anesthesiologist, the oncologist, and the care manager who will oversee all aspects of my surgery. AND they set the surgery date—it will be December 20th.

They expect that they will be able to do the modified Van Nes surgery that will result in me having a prosthetic below the knee. That is good news.

I don't know yet how long I will be in the hospital after the surgery or how long the rehab will be re:

my prosthetic and relearning how to walk, etc. I should have that information after the meetings on the 7th.

I continue to feel confident about the surgery and the fact that the cancer will be gone. Having the opportunity to have the below-the-knee prosthetic will allow me to walk, jog and play golf. I will be a little slower but still able to get around.

Thanks to everyone for your kind words and the posts to the guestbook (CaringBridge). It means more than I can say to hear from everyone.

One of the best responses to that post was from Harry Fullerton who plays with me in my golf league. That league, the Construction League, is comprised of sixty of the nicest and most irreverent men I know. In addition to reminding me that I was in his thoughts and prayers he had a suggestion: "See if they can fix your slice when they fix your leg."

My trip to Boston on December 7 turned out to be a marathon day. I left Portland at 5:30 a.m. to be in Boston by 8:30. Boston rush hour traffic is the real deal. I told people about that day in my next post.

CaringBridge Post
December 10, 2012
What they said about the surgery and recovery
10 days before the surgery

Thanks to everyone for all the kind words and deeds. It is so very touching and humbling to be on the receiving end of all the love and support we have been given.

The trip to Brigham and Women's and Dana Farber (the two hospitals are across the street from one another) was a long day. My sister Bonnie (the smart, focused RN) and I got to BWH at about 8:30 and were meeting with the Vascular Surgeon 15 minutes later. That was the last appointment that was on time all day . . .

In the course of the day I had sonograms of the arteries of both legs, X-rays of both legs, did all the preoperative blood work, labs and an EKG and met with the orthopedic surgeon who will do the operation and my oncologist at Dana Farber.

The last meeting, with the oncologist, was touching because at this point he is not in the medical loop as we prepare for surgery, but he asked if I would stay to see him just because he wanted to check in to see how I was doing and to reassure me that we were taking the best course of action.

The orthopedic surgeon went over all the risks of the surgery and then told us he expected a long (10 hours) but successful surgery. The biggest piece of news for me to digest was that he did not want me to bear weight on the reconstructed hip joint for six months. I was mentally ready to begin learning to use a prosthetic within a month or so after surgery and his words hit pretty hard. Initially six months on crutches seemed like a horribly long time but as I have reflected on it over the weekend, I realize it will probably be the first of several things post-operatively that may change and will require me to adjust, and I will be best served by just accepting those types of things and focusing my efforts on the things I can affect like physical therapy and my day-to-day activities.

I did go online to read Dr. Winkelman's (he is the doctor who invented the variation that they will be using) 1986 paper on the results of his procedure and three of the four people he referenced were bearing weight at four months and the fourth at three months, so my hope is that the doctors at BWH are just being conservative. The surgeon did tell me that as soon as the X-rays show the bones have fused, I will be able to begin learning to walk and that the (fused) joint will be very, very strong.

So, at this point I wait, continue to work to get the first-floor apartment ready for our return and reflect on the wonderful friends that Cindy and I have. Bruce and I will continue our 6:30 a.m.

walks on M-W-F with next Monday being the last one for a while. But we will pick up again when we can after the surgery and hopefully at some time in the summer be able to start jogging again.

Thanks again for all the love and support.

As I wrote those words, in December of 2012, I had no idea what the next six months were going to bring.

The Die Is Cast

I wrote the following poem once we knew the surgery would occur:

The unknown has become known
I know my leg must go to save my life
The die is cast, the action certain
All that remains to be seen is my response

How will I react to the physical change?
The mental uncertainty?
The looks of concern or disgust from others?
How will I handle the now known future?

As I write I know that I must persevere
My future awaits and I can't escape

But how? With grace? Or not?
My hope is that pragmatism prevails while my emotions stay engaged

I must handle the pain
Endure and conquer the boredom
Understand and implement the exercise
I must bring the old me to the new me

I can't control the cancer or the cure
I can control my response to both
Accept the reality and work to make it better
Don't settle for less than the best outcome

Refocus everyday
Rededicate moment by moment
Reinforce the weak part of my effort
And be kind with the inevitable shortfalls

I will be who I make myself. Period.

Handicapped

CaringBridge Post
December 14, 2012
Thinking of some things
6 days before the surgery

As I move closer and closer to the day of my surgery I am thinking about a number of things. Some of the thoughts are what I expected: How much pain will I be in after the surgery? For how long? What will I think and feel when I look down and see my reconstructed, shortened, and rotated leg? When will I walk again? But I have also started to think more broadly about the handicapped people around us.

Technically, I will qualify as handicapped in that I will need adaptations to make my way in the world. As we have remodeled the first-floor bathroom, we are paying attention to handrails and other changes to make it easier for me to get around—the adaptations I will need. As I have thought about joining the ranks of the handicapped, I have become more aware of those with differences around me. I am ashamed to say that often in the past I would see a person with a limp or in a wheelchair and see them only with my eyes but not with my feelings. I viewed them analytically with little or no empathy. Now I look carefully, not only to see what is different physically but also to see the person behind the difference or disability. In six days, I will be one of those people that you see who doesn't look the same, who walks funny or slowly.

I have said in the past that my struggle with cancer has been a blessing as well as a curse. In this instance, as I have been forced to deepen my understanding of the human condition and the diversity it entails, I am a better man for having to face this cancer. I have had to face the limited way that I was living my life emotionally. I wonder how many potentially wonderful moments I have missed because I was unaware of the people and situations around me.

This is ironic as I have a master's degree in adapted physical education. I was trained to work with handicapped and older populations. Maybe that is one reason that I have viewed those handicapped persons analytically. I was able to recognize the particular disability or difference because of my education and training. But I realize now that each person, difference, or disability aside, is an individual just like me. I know that people will look at me differently after the surgery and rehab. I hope they take the time to see me, not just my shortened leg or prosthetic.

Bruce Davis

One of the greatest blessings to come out of my cancer, surgery, and recovery was the knowledge that I had people in my life who were incredibly special. One of those people was my running partner (and good friend) Bruce Davis. I wrote about Bruce in my next post.

CaringBridge Post
December 18, 2012
Walking in the snow
2 days before the surgery

Since May of last year Bruce Davis and I have met at 6:30 a.m. each Monday, Wednesday, and Friday for some morning exercise. We started to meet because I was training to run the L.L.Bean 10K road race on July 4, 2012, and Bruce offered to run the race with me (my sister Bonnie and the wonderful Megan Hopps also ran that race with us).

I had set the goal of running the 10K when I was originally diagnosed with cancer in August of 2011 and the doctors told me they were going to remove most of two of the four big muscles in my thigh when they cut out the cancer. Training for the race became my way of taking control of a situation that in the end, I had no control over; the cancer needed to come out and my leg would never be the same again. However, by training each day I was taking a physical action to fight back against the unseen cancer.

We ran the race, and I ran another 10K a month or so later. After the July Fourth race Bruce and I decided that we would continue to meet each Monday, Wednesday, and Friday for our runs and what had developed into wonderful talks as we ran.

In September of this year, I began to feel some tightness in my thigh that worsened and eventually led to the diagnosis that the cancer had returned. Bruce was a trooper. When I told him it was becoming too painful to run he said, "That's okay we can walk, and if it gets too bad to walk, we can just meet for coffee in the morning."

It never came to coffee, but my walking ability has been slowed as the tumor grew. Monday was our last walk before I leave for Boston on Wednesday.

During the spring and summer, we would run about a 3.5-mile loop along the water on the Eastern Prom trail and then into downtown and back up the hill to the corner of North and Quebec Streets. When I needed to change to a walk, we shortened the route and walked along Fore Street and the Prom. Whether we were running or walking we had many wonderful talks about what was going on in our lives. Bruce was completing his master's degree in social work (as a classmate of Cindy's), his daughter was completing her residency and announcing the birth of another child, I was hard at work building my practice with my partner Eric, we both had vacations to relive; we were rarely at a loss for words. But sometimes as we ran or walked into the sun rising over Casco Bay there wasn't a need for words, the beauty of the view was more than enough.

One morning we met in a dense fog. As we started to run from the top of Munjoy Hill down the path to the water's edge trails it was gray, with no hint of sun. We ran along the trail unable to see more than a hundred feet out into the murky fog over the water. And then, as the sun came over the horizon far out in the bay, the rays of light penetrated below the fog, so the water became a dazzling, dancing field of light while, at a height of fifty feet or so, the fog bank absorbed all the light and the grayness was solid above this amazing light show. It was one of the most spectacular natural displays I have ever seen.

On Monday we acknowledged that this would be the last walk on my own two legs but we both resolved that as soon as I am able, we will continue what has become much more that a three-times-a-week exercise event. Bruce has become a good friend and I am looking forward to putting on a prosthetic limb and walking with him again.

As I write it has been more than eight years since I lost my leg and Bruce and I still meet three times a week. It is a ritual I look forward to and expect to continue if we both are walking on the right side of the grass.

Game On

The CaringBridge site allowed Cindy and I to share what was going on as we navigated this life-altering event. The site also allowed our friends to post their thoughts. On December 19, as I was arriving in Boston for the amputation surgery the next day, Mark and Sue Hilton, friends from my college days at Lyndon State wrote, "Thinking of you tonight—Mark says it is 'game time.' He's watched you play against 6'6" guys and win the battles—succeed at multiple careers—and win the battles. This is another game. GAME ON."

Mark and Sue were correct, it was game time. Cindy, me, and our friends and family had spent the last several months preparing. We had made alterations to our home, we had talked and cried about the unfairness of it all and I had tried to be as physically prepared as I could be in anticipation of the months of rehabilitation I would face. Now the ball was about to be tossed up to begin the next game—the rest of my life game, a game that would change Cindy and I forever. I had the butterflies I had always felt before a game began but these butterflies seemed to be a lot bigger than I remembered them to be.

That night I wrote my last CaringBridge post before the surgery.

CaringBridge Post
December 19, 2012
1 day before the surgery

Cindy, my mother, and I are in Boston and will head to the hospital at 5:30AM tomorrow. My sister Bonnie will be joining Cindy and my mom tomorrow. Cindy will be updating the journal as she has things to report. Thanks to all our friends who have graced us with their love and prayers and those who have helped at the apartment. We are truly blessed.

And with that I laid down and tried to settle my butterflies and sleep. I faced a dawn unlike any I had ever faced or dreamed of. I hoped I was up for the challenge.

The next morning, we arrived on time and almost immediately I was taken to the pre-operative suite. I was focused as I talked with the orthopedic surgeon, the vascular surgeon, the anesthesiologist, and their support staff. I was keenly aware of the procedures around me as IVs were placed in both arms and I was prepped for the central intravenous lines that would be placed in my neck and my chest once I was unconscious on the operating room table. Then the left side my stomach, pelvis, left leg, and chest were shaved. When

I asked why they were shaving my chest the nurse pointed out that they wanted to be ready in case anything should go wrong while I was on the operating table.

Yet at the same time as I interacted with the doctors and their staff as we prepared for what would ultimately be a twenty-hour surgery my mind slipped back to a time and place thirty years earlier. I was back at Lyndon State and we were playing Plymouth State College from neighboring New Hampshire. As I lay on that gurney in Brigham and Women's Hospital waiting for my leg to be cut off and reattached in a Frankenstein-type of operation, I was fifty-three years old, decades removed from my college-playing days and the highlight moment that was playing in my mind.

I could see and hear the atmosphere inside our gymnasium. It was a typical small college game, maybe 500 or 600 fans watching on a cold winter night in northern New England. It was a hard-fought game, as all our games with Plymouth were. Their campus was just ninety minutes down the highway, our coaches knew each other well, and many of us players had competed against each other in high school and in summer leagues.

The pace of the game was quick as both teams worked hard to fast-break on every opportunity and the defense was intense with each pass and catch contested. I felt alive as I ran the floor, defended, blocked out, and struggled with everyone else to do everything I could to help my team win.

The play I was reliving from my gurney, attached to IVs and surrounded by the surgical staff, began as my old prep school roommate and current teammate, Mike Whaley, stepped between two Plymouth State players and made a steal. He gathered the ball and streaked down the floor for an uncontested layup. Normally, I would have watched as Mike laid the ball in for an easy two points. But this night I felt compelled to run and follow what I assumed to be an easy play for my teammate.

As I ran after Mike and closed the distance between him and the goal he was heading toward, one of the Plymouth players nearly caught Mike as he was beginning his shot. Mike slightly bobbled the ball and missed the layup. The ball hit the backboard and caromed off the rim, high and to the left. I jumped, timed it, grabbed the ball with both hands, and dunked it back through the hoop. Our bench exploded and the crowd came to attention. These types of plays didn't happen too often in our league and everyone, including me, was savoring the moment.

Everyone, that is, except Al Lacroix. Al was the lead official on the play and as he looked up from his baseline position, underneath the goal, he thought I had grabbed the ball while it was still in the imaginary cylinder above the rim and waived the play off. I tried to explain that from his point of view almost any play like the one I made would look like goaltending and that I had waited for the ball to clear the cylinder before cramming it back through. Like most arguments with officials, I ended up on the losing end of this one.

As I lay on the gurney, this hyper-athletic play was in my mind and I was glad that I had the legs, skill, and drive to make that play long ago. Al Lacroix was wrong—but it didn't matter.

At a little after 7:30 the team in the pre-op suite said it was time to go. I was given a mild sedative through my left arm IV and we started to roll down a narrow hall to the operating suite.

When we arrived at the operating room, I was struck by two things: it was a relatively small room stuffed with people and equipment; and it was very cold. They placed my gurney next to the hard, narrow operating table and I helped them slide me into place. As soon as I was on my back staring at the bright white ceiling the whole affair became very real. I wasn't panicked, probably because of the narcotics the anesthesiologist began to administer. As I relaxed more, I remember a nurse taking my left arm and strapping it down on the cross-shaped support. As she moved to my right side and began to strap that arm in place, I remember thinking that this was a bit claustrophobic . . . In truth I never finished that thought as I slipped under the anesthesia.

Surgery

CaringBridge Post (Cindy)
December 20, 2012 • 4:42 p.m.
From Cindy
In surgery for a little over 9 hours

Hi everyone. I just got a call from John's doctor. He says that John is doing well and that his vitals are stable. He also said that they sent the distal tissue (the far end of tumor in the muscle tissue) to pathology and it came back clean, so they are continuing with the operation as planned. He said the operation would take a couple more hours. Thank you all for hanging in there with us. I will let you know more when I do but it is good news.

* * *

CaringBridge Post (Cindy)
December 20, 2012 • 7:26 p.m.
Me again
In surgery 12 hours

Well, I got a little tired of waiting. When I asked, they said he was still in surgery which did not satisfy me, so I asked them to call the OR. They did and I spoke with the OR nurse—Cat—who said that John is doing very well and that the reason it is taking so long because they are being very methodical and taking great care and going slowly. She said that the vascular surgeon has not even begun his work yet and that it will take him a while—so it looks like a few more hours. She promised me that him being under anesthesia for this long is not harmful to him—but it looks like it's gonna be a long night!! I'll update again but it may be when some of you are asleep. XO

CaringBridge Post (Cindy)
December 21, 2012 • 1:52 a.m.
He is out of surgery

And I have now been up for 24 hours so please excuse my brevity. Operation was 20 hours. He came through like a champ. Doctor said it took so long because he is so healthy and works out so much that he had developed many more veins and vessels than someone who isn't as healthy as he is. He is still asleep and won't be awake until tomorrow. His color is great. Foot looks good. Going to see him one more time and then off to bed.

CaringBridge Post (Cindy)
December 21, 2012 • 8:55 a.m.
Morning everyone

John is doing well. He was transfused (adding blood) only once during the night which is good. They are working on getting the breathing tube out today—which is quick, but he is so strong he is breathing over the respirator. His color is great and he is holding our hands and responding to commands and answering questions—by nodding. All a little ahead of schedule—because you know our John—he is an overachiever!! He (and we) will be happy when that breathing tube is out. We (Cindy and my mother) are just back to the hotel for the first time in over 24 hours to shower and nap and back we go. We are taking shifts, so he is never alone although I plan to stay most of the time. The first big step is done . . . onward and upward. Our love to all.

The Other Side

Before the surgery, the doctors made clear that they would not know until they began the operation whether they could execute the rotationplasty or whether they would have to take my entire leg (because the combination of the cancer and the anatomy wouldn't allow for the rotationplasty). A good result would leave me with a shortened, backward facing leg. A bad outcome would leave me with nothing below my hip on my left side. I would not know until I awoke from the surgery.

When I became fully aware in the intensive care unit, I didn't know it was over thirty-six hours since I remembered slipping away on the operating room table. After the almost twenty hours in surgery the doctors had kept me lightly sedated as they slowly brought me to consciousness to allow me to rest and to allow them to monitor my recovery from the loss of blood during the surgery, the transfusions afterward, and any lingering effects of the long time I had spent under the strong anesthesia required for the surgery.

I don't remember interacting with Cindy or my sister, Bonnie, or my mother until I became fully aware of the breathing tube down my throat. At that point I was alert and looked down to see the shortened left leg underneath the sheet—the operation had been a success! Next on my agenda was getting off the respirator so I could stop choking and begin communicating.

Cindy tells me that during my last night in the ICU I told her that we were going to have to take this "one step at a time" and I smiled and said, "Pun intended."

CaringBridge Post (Cindy)
December 22, 2012
Hi everyone
2 days after the surgery

John is out of ICU and in a private room. He "walked" with a walker forty feet today. They are still working on a good pain control cocktail and it is going well: some of the time he makes perfect sense—other times not so much. Many of you have said that's normal for him anyway!

We have a friend, Mia, who is having a baby. Every day he opens his eyes and asks, "Mia?" and I say, "No, not today." Today he said "Mia?" and I said, "No, not today." And he said I was mistaken—that she had her baby and was with Somalis. He thought about it for a minute and then said, "That statement was an error, wasn't it?"

He also asked his sister to leave the room and stand outside for a minute . . . he thought he asked her to come back in, but he never said it out loud. He does that a little too . . . he thinks he says something, but he only thought it. It makes for interesting conversations.

I keep forgetting what day it is. Someone finally told me the date and I thought, "That's great but is it Friday, Saturday or Sunday?" It's its own little world down here. John is getting very good care and the doctor said he could be home in three to five days!

Thank you all for your Kindness . . . Cindy

That post received dozens of responses from our friends and family but two stood out because they came from opposite ends of the age spectrum. Patrick Hilton, son of our friends Mark and Sue was in his early twenties, finishing up his MBA when he wrote, "Mr. LeMieux, I am relieved to hear things went as well as they did. I'll make sure to keep up to date. Thinking of you—Patrick." Our good friends Mike and Judy True passed along a message from Judy's mother, Philomena, who was in her early nineties. "She said to tell you both that she says a rosary every night for John! He is special to her." It is impossible to overstate how uplifting and supportive all the posts and messages we received were to us. As I was slowly becoming settled and aware, fighting my way through the narcotic haze of the pain meds, these messages gave me so much inspiration.

The next afternoon I wrote my first post.

> CaringBridge Post
> December 23, 2012
> John's post-op post
> *3 days after the surgery*
>
> So, here I am with Cindy at my side. I have a 16th floor room and a very good PT coordinator. I walked a little over 120' today with my walker and my coach Jill supporting me. Thanks everyone one [*sic*] fo [*sic*] all the very kind and supportive word [*sic*].

I guess I was still fighting my way through the pain meds.

These first days were long and hard for me and for Cindy, my mother, and Bonnie. I was in a fair amount of pain and literally couldn't get comfortable as I had to lie still on my back with as little movement as possible. Except when I suddenly had to go to the bathroom, and everyone mobilized to help me move the fifteen feet from the bed to the toilet! Cindy and my mother and my sister were always with me—supportive, kind and loving. More than I deserved.

I had a tough couple of days on Christmas Eve and Christmas Day with blood level issues and Cindy kept everyone in the loop.

CaringBridge Post (Cindy)
December 24, 2012
Merry Christmas Eve
4 days after the surgery

Hi everyone. John is doing well. He lay on his stomach for fifteen minutes for the first time and he walked with crutches for the first time, so it has been a big day.

Our "other" crazy friends Deb and Steve Jordan came for a visit today which was nice. It looks like we are coming home on Wednesday—John via ambulance.

We are thankful and blessed to have you all in our lives. Have a safe and happy holiday.

John and Cindy

CaringBridge Post (Cindy)
December 25, 2012
Merry Christmas
5 days after the surgery

Hope everyone had a wonderful holiday and enjoyed time with friends and family. It's just what Mum Carlena and I did, roaming the halls of what we in the know call "The Brigham."

John continues to recover well and received one more transfusion last night. John says he is surprised by the amount of pain but that the drugs are doing a good job of chasing it off. Today was more time on crutches, trips to the bathroom and getting more comfortable with his backward facing foot.

The nurses continue to be impressed and say he is ahead of schedule. Returning home tomorrow remains a possibility but we have to wait and see. As you may guess- staff is minimal on Christmas Day. Thank one and all for your kind words and support.

John and Cindy

Getting Home

Starting on December 26 I began to feel a bit more like myself. I was still trapped in this new paradigm where I couldn't move without assistance and I still struggled with the visual of my left foot, facing backward, opposite my right knee. The foot was in a new place, it was still me, but it wasn't where it was supposed to be. Because the leg and foot were facing backward, when I tried to move the foot with intention i.e., point my toes in or out, or circle my ankle, my movements didn't match what I was seeing. Inside was now outside and vice versa. I could make the foot move, but I couldn't control the movements. The foot just kind of jerked and moved in fits and starts. The first time I saw myself in a full-length mirror I was shocked by my foot hanging limp on my left side.

In small, incremental ways I was beginning to come to grips with me after losing my leg. There was every expectation the cancer was gone although I would need five years of clean MRIs and CT scans before the doctors would give me an all clear. I knew the trade-off was the only one I could make. My leg for my life was the bargain of the century but at this point I was too focused on making it through a day five or ten minutes at a time to be too philosophical.

CaringBridge Post
December 26, 2012
John logs in
6 days after the surgery

This morning I had a great set of conversations with my orthopedic surgeon, the anesthesiologist from the operation, a vascular surgeon who assisted on the operation and [*sic*] women [*sic*] who is heading up my physical therapy team.

My progress continues to encourage everyone. The operation was, as we all know by now, long, and arduous. The surgical team did a great job. My now [*sic*] is to make sure the grafted leg heals correctly. At present my leg is held on by eight screws between my hip bone and my lower thigh bone and is sutured on in one continuous loop from the top of my leg all the way around to the back and to the front again. All the screws and sutures need to bind to the bone and flesh for this leg to function properly.

. . . for this to happen I must lie still for a lot of the time. Mostly on my back but occasionally on my stomach, with the attached leg extended but not bearing any weight or affected by gravity. I can get up to go to the bathroom or walk on my crutches a bit mut [*sic*] mostly I am to lie still. I think of it as a very focused lack of motion!

From this morning's discussions we all decided to get X-rays, examine the sutures, and run some other tests tomorrow morning, evaluate all the tests tomorrow afternoon and plan on an early release the next day. Cindy is working with the care coordination RN re: transportation and other issues.

This has already been an incredible journey with all our family [*sic*] friends who have supported us so deeply and securely. Your thoughts, prayers and posts mean so much more than we can articulate. Thank you all for your love and support.

Back to counting the number of indentations on a single 2′ by 2′ ceiling tile!

Love, John

I was not able to go home the next day as had been planned and it wasn't until December 28, eight days after the amputation, that I found myself in a cold ambulance with a very bad suspension making the return trip to Portland, Maine. As I bounced along the Boston streets and on to Route 1 and then Interstate 95 headed north, I was reflecting on two things: First, how was it an ambulance didn't have a heating system or enough blankets to keep me warm? And second, how nice it would be to just settle in at home. Eventually the rocking of the road and my pain medicine allowed me to drop off to sleep.

I arrived home and was transferred to the queen-size bed we had set up in our first-floor apartment. Our friend Steve Jordan was finishing up some of the last electrical work when we arrived and it was good to see him again. His daughter Mia had delivered her son by then and Steve was an excited grandpa.

I met with a visiting nurse to be examined and arrange for the daily visits to attend to my wounds and pain meds. I then went to sleep, and Cindy and my mother also laid down for some well-deserved rest.

Resilience

On Monday, February 15, 1982, our small bus with fewer than twenty passengers pulled out of Lyndon State College for the two-hour-and forty-five-minute drive to Rindge, New Hampshire, to play Franklin Pierce College. The Franklin Pierce Ravens were the two-time defending champion in NAIA District 5 and would win their third title in a row in several weeks. As we headed south on Interstate 91, I was up near the front of the bus trying to convince Skip that we needed to change our game plan if we wanted any chance to win. I was Lyndon's tallest starter at six-two and I would be guarding the Raven's six-nine center Joe Delancy. Their best player was six-three, 220-pound all-American guard Larry Leach. They had six-foot-five forwards and a deep bench. In short, we were short. And not as talented. Finally, Skip turned to me and said, "What do you want me to do? Put in a new offense in the locker room before the game? We are who we are."

I proved prescient in my forecast as Franklin Pierce beat us 138–85. Delancy scored over thirty points including the thousandth of his career, thanks mostly to me. Leach and the others did their thing. It was a classic beatdown.

Two days later, on Wednesday, February 17, the Ravens came to us. We were playing in front of a packed house as the students and townspeople came out to see one of the top teams in New England . . . our opponent! As expected, they were cocky and they had every right to be after the schooling they had given us only two nights before.

Skip had talked in practice the day before about us being who we were and reminding us that we could play too. The game was a war from the beginning as both teams realized things were different than before. We made one small change and I set up in the high post and drifted out to the wings to force the six-nine Delancy to come out from the hoop and try to defend me on the perimeter. That change, some good shooting and poise down the stretch allowed us to leave that night with a 90–86 win. I scored twenty points on Delancy in one of my best college games.

The takeaway from the two games was straightforward: Be who you are and don't let the past predicate the present. On Wednesday we stayed in the moment, made the plays we needed to and came out on top.

As I lay in my bed, with my backward leg attached by screws and sutures, with post-surgical drainage tubes coming through my skin, my lower body wrapped in gauze like a mummy and unable to even roll over without thinking first, I realized that the past had nothing to do with the present. Physically I was as weak as a kitten and everything I had ever known about myself as an athlete or even as a person—how

I went through the world, was in question. I had a new set of challenges in front of me and the only way I was going to succeed was to figure out who I was and what I needed to do now.

New Year's and New Paradigm

CaringBridge Post
December 29, 2012
First full day at home
9 days after the surgery

It is almost 9 p.m. and we are wrapping up our first full day at home. Cindy has been busy with reorganizations we need to do to have me be comfortable on the first floor. While Cindy was working my mom was helping me with meals, pills, etc.

I met with both a wound care nurse (one comes every day to change the dressing on my 360-degree sutures and tend to the small bits of skin that require attention following the surgery) and the physical therapist.

We also had several visitors, and it was good to catch up with folks by phone as well. One thing that has been made clear to me is that we have been blessed with the greatest group of friends! The outpouring of love, support, and friendship we have experienced is deeply touching.

My job over the next five to six months is to stay focused on keeping my rebuilt left hip and thigh as static as possible. I need to give the new hip joint (joined by eight screws) every opportunity to fuse. The more movement that I make the more opportunity for the fusion to be delayed or interrupted. I spend twenty-two to twenty-four hours per day on my back or on my stomach. While the rest feels good now after the hectic last nine days, it will take a lot of concentration to not move as time goes by. I have discovered this already. While going through the giant pile of mail that was waiting for us at home I inadvertently moved into a sitting position—expressly what the surgeon had said not to do! I caught myself and slid down to a more reclined position. It is strange to not be trying to be up and active ASAP.

I will take the next week and do nothing and then we will move my office to my bed, and I will work from my back and/or stomach. I can read research, review accounts, and talk to clients without moving. That's the plan. I will have several follow-up appointments at Dana Farber/Brigham and Women's over the next several weeks and will follow instructions to the letter. I hope to have the bone fusion happen as soon as possible to allow me to begin rehab with a prosthetic as soon as possible. This boring, critical part of the process must be done and done well.

All our love and thanks, John and Cindy.

I didn't post again until New Year's Eve as I laid still, slept, and tried to develop the appetite that had been suppressed by the pain meds I was on. I spent most of my time by myself as Cindy and my mother were also recovering from their own stress of supporting me and each other through the surgery and its immediate aftermath. They were exhausted from days of being there for me, responding to whatever I needed and living in a hospital room, eating hospital food, and sleeping only when my schedule allowed. My sister, Bonnie, a registered nurse, was trying to help me replace the narcotic pain medication with sufficient over-the-counter combinations that would knock down the pain without making me drowsy (or constipated). Eventually we discovered a combination of Tylenol and Advil that stayed within the limits for daily use and kept my pain at bay—that was a game changer.

As December 31 dawned, I was awake and thinking about the fact that for the last twelve or thirteen years we had spent New Year's Eve and New Year's Day with our good friends Deb and Steve Jordan. Either we go to their house or they come to ours and we have the same routine each year.

On New Year's Eve we eat a meal that Cindy prepared: a scallop and crabmeat quiche and her mother's lobster stew followed by a decadent dessert and coffee (and maybe a scotch or two) as we talk and laugh our way to midnight. We save our Christmas presents and exchange those after dinner. Cindy and Deb have the same large gift bag—after more than a decade it is now held together with tape and string—that they rotate each year as the "wrapping" for their present. The next morning, we wake up late and Steve and I make a big brunch with eggs, potatoes, meat, and pancakes. We relax, go for a walk, and chat until it is time to head home in the early afternoon.

This year there would be no quiche or stew or brunch.

CaringBridge Post
December 31, 2012
New Year's Eve
11 days after the surgery

As I prepare to go to sleep almost four hours before the ball drops, I have been struck quite directly by the enormity of my situation and at the same time by the equally enormous resources I have in the form of my loving wife, family, and friends.

This year will be unlike anything Cindy or I have experienced. The challenges ahead are daunting. I frankly don't know how I will manage to be as still as I need to be. But somehow, I will do it.

Traditionally, folks make resolutions on New Year's Eve; the things we want to do differently to make our lives better. My resolution this year is quite simple: I want to do the best I can to get better, I want to treat Cindy with the love she deserves, and I will pay forward the love and support I have received throughout this entire experience.

Here is to a 2013 filled with family, friends, sharing and caring for one another.

John

Back to Boston

I was able to spend the first week at home as planned, resting and recovering—beginning to figure out what my new life might be like. I was in bed, either reclining on my back or lying on my stomach all day, every day, except to get up to make my way, with assistance, to the bathroom. My mom and Cindy brought me meals and my meds and made sure I was okay. On January 2, after five days at home we had a post-operative appointment with the surgeon:

> CaringBridge Post
> January 3, 2013
> At Brigham & Women's follow-up yesterday
> *14 days after the surgery*
>
> Cindy and I went down to BWH yesterday to meet with our surgeon for a follow-up appointment. The appointment went very well, he likes the way everything looks, and we are going back next week

to see him again to have a surgical drain removed and some of the sutures taken out.

The real story is how we got to Boston. Throughout all my illness with cancer my sister Bonnie has been at my side and made every trip to Dana Farber or Brigham & Women's with me. Because the doctor's office changed the date and time of yesterday's appointment, she could not make the trip. I asked several people who had larger SUVs to see who may have been able to drive me down, as Cindy, like a lot of folks doesn't like to drive in Boston. The response from our friends, as it has been every time we have had a need was tremendous.

We had several offers of vehicles and drivers but the one that worked out best was that my cousin Lance and his wife (also named Cindy LeMieux) made their SUV available although both had to work; so, my friend Drew Juris rearranged his day and did the driving. We filled the passenger seat footwell with pillows to support my short leg, laid the seat all the way back and I had a comfortable and well-supported posture for the trip.

As I mentioned above, the doctor was happy with my progress but for me the highlight of the trip was the trip itself. It felt so good to be out and about, to see the bright snow and blue sky and just watch the people on the road and at the hospital.

I am working to determine how I am going to make my way through this forced period of inactivity. It is not always easy. I am by nature very independent (some may say too independent) and now I find myself very dependent on others. It is both a humbling and an educational experience. I don't know how I could not come out of this experience a better man. I am learning so much about myself and my relationship with others every day.

Cindy and my mom have been a tremendous support as I have resettled back at home. They have been unwavering in their physical, mental, and emotional support and I could not have made it this far without them.

To all my incredibly supportive friends and family, your love, kind words and actions have changed me forever.

Shared History

A couple of weeks after my surgery my longtime friend and prep school and college teammate Mike Whaley came to visit. I was resting in bed when I heard his voice in the hall. I couldn't wait to see him. While everyone else who had visited me since the surgery had pulled up one of the two chairs in the room, Mike came right in and sat on the edge of my bed. At that point we had known each other for thirty-six years and while we don't see each other more than four or five times a year, we have a relationship that goes beyond words. He was the best man at my first wedding when we both just kids of twenty-four, and he had seen the best and worst of me in the decades since. Mike was (and remains today) the most interesting combination of pragmatism and empathy. He calls the world as he sees it and he sees it more clearly than most.

We talked about my surgery and my forced, prone recovery. We caught up about old college friends and what he was doing now in his job as the sports editor of a regional newspaper. As he was getting ready to go, he told me that on the morning of my surgery he had been thinking about my put-back dunk against Plymouth State all those years ago. As I lay on that operating room table, we were a hundred miles apart and more than thirty years removed from that day on the court at Lyndon State, yet we had shared that moment again.

Moments in Time

CaringBridge Post
January 7, 2013
Day-to-day realities
18 days after the surgery

As I have realized and said many times, the support that Cindy and I have received from our friends and family through my ordeal has been and continues to be wonderful.

Many of you have written or told me how strong I am and how well I am dealing with this stunningly life-changing event. I appreciate all the support, prayers, and kind words but I wanted to write to be totally honest about my early rehabilitation experiences.

First, I do think I am dealing rather well with this

reality overall. But I would be lying to say that there have not been dark moments, hours, and even large parts of days, when I felt overwhelmed by the enormity and irreversible nature of the surgery, my rehab and my life going forward.

Nothing will ever be the same. That doesn't mean that the future will be bad, but it certainly will be different than the life I knew before my leg was cut off.

I am coming to grips everyday with the limitations I currently have and those that I will have for the rest of my life. It is scary sometimes because I was a very independent person and now, at least in the first five to six months of this rehab, I need help with almost everything I do. I know that once I get my hip fused and begin to use a prosthetic, I will be closer to my action-oriented self as I learn to walk and learn to use the new leg.

Today was a good example. I was up early and had a good breakfast before my home health aide and the nurses to tend to my surgical wound came to care for me. I had work lined up to do and (my business partner) Eric brought over some paper-work to sign.

At some point early in the afternoon I began to feel overwhelmed by the fact that I needed to be

> reclined and that I struggle to move and change into new postures that are really only variations of previous postures. There are only so many ways one can lie down!
>
> Talking with Cindy helps, and we have developed plans to help me cope with the ups and downs that I know are going to come. My highs still far outweigh my lows, and I am committed to take advantage of this opportunity to learn much about myself. I will be better on the other side I know is coming.

This post was the first time I had reflected openly about the anxiety that was a companion through much of my rehabilitation. Talking with Cindy did help but this was a scary, new emotion that wasn't going away. Around the same time, I wrote the following essay reflecting on anxiety and my life.

Moments in Time

I played basketball at a small college in Vermont in the late seventies and early eighties. There are wonderful moments in close basketball games where time seems to slow and the game is simply one full second . . . and then the next . . . and then the next one after that. As you play you can see the five players on offense moving together and the five defenders anticipating and reacting as if matching actors in a carefully choreographed scene.

In those moments, every pass and catch matters. You must come meet every pass or your defender steps to the ball and takes it from you. You play at full speed and rip and tear and elbow and lean to gain your advantage, as does he. Getting your man to lean just a bit to the right gives you the opening you need to push with your shoulder and force the space to go left. You play with a raw physical abandon that is on the edge of being wild but always under control; where the defense rotates to meet your move and take away the advantage you barely gained one second earlier. And you pass to your teammate left open by the defender who rotates to you and the ballet continues until someone—hopefully the other team—can't recover and the advantage leads to a score.

Even then all that happens is that the ballet moves to the other end of the floor with the players continuing to search and parry for that split second where you either outhustle or outwit or outbalance the other guy. You win that moment or sometimes he does, but in any case, the beautiful give-and-take continues.

This wonderful stretching of time can last for minutes as the collective concentration on the floor forces everyone, all ten players and even the referees to play the game at its purest. When play stops for a time-out or a foul call all you want is to be back in action, seeking to force your will on your opponent and win each special moment until the clock expires with your team in the lead.

When I came home from the hospital and began the early stages of the enforced bed rest that needed to happen for the screwed-together bones in my hip to fuse I was living in the opposite of those precious moments I had enjoyed thirty years earlier. I faced nothing but time and there were no teammates or opponents to play the game with me. The game was entirely in my head and I needed to find a way to force myself to do what needed to be done.

During the first four months after my surgery, before the knee joint that had been reversed and transplanted to my hip had firmly grown to be one with the bones of my pelvis, the doctors made it clear that if I put any weight on those articulating bones that were held together with only eight titanium screws, the bones could separate and I would lose even the shortened misshapen leg I had. Putting weight on the hip included sitting up. I was required to lie on my back or my stomach. For four months I couldn't sit up more than fifteen degrees.

I came home with two surgical drains attached to rubber collection bulbs that slowly filled each day with the bloody fluids that were still flowing in the wounded area. I had bandages that wrapped around my waist and looped down and circled my rear end and the newly attached leg and the 360 degrees of stitches that held my skin and tissue together. I lay on my back staring at the ceiling or my stomach looking at a wall for far longer than I thought possible.

As those early days at home followed one after the

other, I alternated between mind-numbing boredom and heart-pounding anxiety. I was literally trapped. I was forbidden to move. Period. Everything I had always held to be true about myself; that I was strong and athletic and in control, was lost. I was as weak as a toddler. I couldn't even roll over without thought and preparation and in no universe was I in control. I experienced waves of crippling anxiety. I was attacked from within with the new uncertainties I faced. *Will the pain stop? Would my leg heal? Will I be able to walk? Run? How will people react to me when they see me on the street?* While all these thoughts were always present the anxiety came like a storm, independent of any thought or feeling I could recognize. I would be lying in bed and then, in seconds, the anxiety would envelope my body and my mind. I was gasping for breath, crying out loud without control and compelled to move to try and dissipate the forces that were attacking me.

But I couldn't move. I was trapped.

As time went on Cindy helped me with coping strategies. As a clinical therapist she had the understanding to support me. I learned to see the anxiety as something that wanted to visit me, not as part of me. I became able to recognize the very earliest symptoms of the anxiety as it tried to settle within my body. I could feel my breath become faster and shallow. I could sense the muscles in my head and neck and chest begin to tighten. I became able to slow things down and anticipate my opponent's moves just like I did when I played as that young college ballplayer thirty years prior in those games in small college gyms on cold winter nights. I learned to dance with my anxiety and seek my advantage. Most of the time I was able to force anxiety to yield to me and to give me just enough space so I could make the emotional moves I needed to keep myself together. Sometimes, just like my old college games, the anxiety won. Those hours felt longer than the others. But more and more, as I got into better emotional shape, I prevailed.

Stoicism

CaringBridge Post
January 9, 2013
One happy doctor
20 days after the surgery

We just returned from an appointment with Dr. Marco Ferrone at Brigham and Women's Hospital. Paul Johnson (who was a professor of Cindy's in her undergraduate work and whose wife Peg is the office manager at Anton LeMieux Financial Group) graciously drove Cindy and me down to Boston, providing safe transportation, good conversation and a well-reasoned mind as we discussed the next steps of my situation.

We started our appointment with an extensive set of X-rays. Dr. Ferrone explained that the radiographic evidence trails actual healing by two to three weeks, and he was pleased that the X-rays showed no change from the post-surgical pictures. That means healing is happening.

The big news is that he removed the last surgical drain and removed ALL my sutures. It finally feels like the surgery itself is over now that the stitches are out and the drain is gone. I left the hospital on a natural high!

Most of the sutures came out without any tugging or pain. We did have a funny moment when he was removing a stitch located low on my rear end. As he cut and pulled the suture out, I felt a strong pinch. I looked over my shoulder and said, "If anyone is going to pinch my butt I hope they wouldn't look like you." His retort: "The way your butt looks now you are lucky to have anyone pinch it!"

He is pleased with the healing that has already occurred and strongly reminded me to continue with the protocol of staying still (on my back or front) as much of the time as I can. I will see him again in early February.

The feeling of being free of the sutures and the Xeroform and gauze that covered them is wonderful. Not having to be aware of the surgical drain as I stand, scoot or roll over is liberating. I can take a shower tomorrow afternoon, another milestone, and a liberating event.

I am in the process of developing a workable schedule to allow me to get the supine rest I need each day, the physical therapy work I need to do for my arms and back, the time I need to do the work I can for Anton LeMieux (Financial Group) clients and time to spend with my friends and family. I am sure it will take several iterations until I get it right but eventually, I will have a workable, repeatable schedule to help me get the most out of each day.

I am also writing down my thoughts as I experience them so I can look back on this experience to help recognize what I was feeling at each moment along the way.

Another thought has been with me today. In the last couple of weeks, while I have had the surgery we all have followed, close friends of Cindy and mine have lived the full spectrum of life. Some of our friends have experienced the tragic, too-early deaths of family members while others have celebrated the birth of a grandchild. Far too often, I am focused only on what is going on with me while life goes on around me.

I will certainly need to continue to do all I can to

battle through the day-to-day ups and downs of my recovery, but I am reminded that . . . as big as my surgery and recovery is, it is just a part of everyday life.

The Roman philosopher Seneca the Younger lived from 4BC to 65AD. Along with the later philosopher Epictetus, Seneca espoused Stoicism, an approach to living that teaches that the path to *eudaimonia* (contentment or happiness) is found by accepting the moment as it presents itself. Stoics believed that virtue (knowing ourselves) is, itself, an end to be sought and that outside influences such as other people, events, wealth, or poverty are not good or bad in and of themselves but are available as substance for virtue to act upon. They theorized that by using our mind and our will to step back from the moment, we can see ourselves and our lives through a longer lens, as part of a greater whole. The goal should be not to be controlled by the desire for pleasure or fear of pain but to use the mind to comprehend the world and see ourselves as part of nature's unfolding plan. By removing ourselves from the emotion of a moment or what someone says about us, we get to decide what is sincerely important to us and how we choose to react (or not to react at all). The assumption that we know why someone does or says something or why a particular thing happens to us or a family member is a fallacy. We cannot know the mind or intentions of another person or why some tragedy befalls us. We do, however, choose our response.

In his *Moral Letters*, Seneca writes, "Let every day, as soon as it comes, be welcome as being the choicest, and let it be made our own possession. We must catch that which flees."

The only thing we control is the moment we find ourselves in. The past, in and of itself, cannot affect the present nor can the future help us in any way. We can and should learn from the past to help us with our reactions to the present so we can have a better future. We must capture and explore and utilize the day we have as time stands still for no man.

Another saying that the great coach John Wooden repeated often was to "make each day your masterpiece." . . . What will I do today to make the best use of the twenty-four hours I have been granted? The poet, writer, and actor Rene Ricard put it more simply in 1982 when he was thirty-six years old: "I had to make my history quick because there would be no future, merely a gossamer world blown about on the zeitgeist, till zeitgeist, the wind of the times, is blasted away by kamikaze, the wind of God."

Emotional Action

In January of 2013 I wrote the following essay for myself. I didn't share it on the CaringBridge site.

Only One Path

Regarding the rehabilitation process I really have no choice as to what my future will be. I do have choices as to how I proceed through that future.

I have two time frames to deal with. The bone fusion time frame; six months, maybe less, until my rebuilt left hip becomes strong enough to bear weight. And the prosthetic time frame—after the fusion, when I am fitted with and learn to utilize my artificial leg.

The second phase is more comfortable to me emotionally because I have always been better at setting and executing physical goals than I have at accepting and dealing with emotional realities. I learned as a boy to disassociate from tough times by taking some action; be it retreating into the fantasy world of a new book or later going to the court and working out until I was exhausted and my emotions had settled. As an adult I could still just go for a run or head to the driving range to focus on anything except the emotional issue at hand. I am particularly good at putting my emotions at arm's length and then just letting the moment pass without too closely addressing the important emotional component.

But in the first phase of my rehabilitation, I am forced to physical inaction. My job is to be as still as I can to allow the new hip to fuse. My wife, who not only knows me better than anyone else but is also a trained clinical therapist, has pointed out that I have a unique opportunity that will not be mine again.

I have the gift of these next five to six months to address the emotional component of my life in a day-to-day manner. To take each day and face the reality. I don't have a choice as to what I will do physically but I have a multitude of choices as to how I will make my way emotionally. I can come to grips with the unrelenting reality that my leg is gone and figure out how I feel about that.

How I really feel: sad about the loss of my physical leg; scared about the loss of my independence and the new need to rely on others for the next six months; fear that my life will change in ways I can't imagine; and concern about the financial strain my rehabilitation may place upon my business and our personal lives.

I have the gift of facing, recognizing, and accepting

my emotions. For the first time in my life I can't leave or change or move to avoid the unpleasantness in front of me. My opportunity is to seize this chance to face the emotions I have spent my whole life dodging. It is a scary and threatening possibility. But it is a great chance to grow and become a much stronger and more complete person.

I did write a post that summarized my thoughts.

CaringBridge Post
January 14, 2013
Emotional education
25 days after the surgery

One of the most compelling things to come out of this surgery and rehab so far, has been the increased attention I have had to give to my emotions. For all my life I have been very action-oriented. I was the guy you wanted there in an emergency, but I never learned to process what I was feeling. I just went on to the next thing.

When I was younger, I disappeared into the make-believe land of a book and as I got older and discovered athletics, I would go for a long run or shoot a couple hundred jump shots when my emotions started to weigh on me.

Now, I have the time and increasingly the

willingness to face the emotions attached to my situation. I face the duality of knowing that I will be better as I come out the other side of this situation while in the meantime, I face an anxiety that attacks because I feel trapped in this lack-of-movement scenario.

The opportunity to sit with the reality of my emotions and learn to accept what I can't change is the opportunity to grow from the inside out. Accepting what I can't change is difficult because all my life I have just moved on to the next thing when the present got too emotionally tough. Now, I can't just move on physically and more importantly, I want to move through what I feel. I think the chance to learn more about myself is going to make me a better person, more empathetic and able to do more for those around me.

Angels and Acceptance

Coming to grips with the reality of losing my leg was an exercise in incremental acceptance. I knew, of course, that the amputation was necessary to save my life. Cancer doesn't rest quietly in its host. It attacks and spreads and disables and kills. But knowing is not the same as doing or being able to live at peace with the new paradigm. Peace for me came slowly, fitfully, and like a jigsaw puzzle with a couple of missing pieces, I struggled to put it all together.

As the years have unfolded, I have become more comfortable with the way I look. It doesn't bother me when people look at me or when they ask questions. I don't mind explaining why my prosthesis looks the way it does or why there is an extra bump in the back of my leg (my toes, in my prosthetic, face backward at knee level). I am okay with letting people know I lost my leg to cancer versus the war injury that many assume. The cosmetic and social aspects of losing my leg and making my way in a biped world are certainly easier.

What has lingered is the absence of simply grabbing my shoes and going for a run or a casual game of tennis or beach volleyball with family. That loss, the loss of moving without thinking and reacting to a tossed ball or reaching quickly for an item high on a shelf, is with me every moment of every day. It is inescapable. There are so many things I can't do physically—athletically really. Even the things I can do require thought and patience on my part and a willingness to go slower or accommodate my needs in other, different ways from my hiking partners (most often Cindy) or golfing friends.

For example, climbing a step ladder to change a lightbulb requires planning and caution. It is difficult for me to even stand on my tiptoes to reach an item up high. Whereas before I would just do it, now I stop and analyze what might go wrong so I don't put myself or those around me at a disadvantage or in danger.

At times I will see someone jogging around Back Cove in my hometown, taking advantage of a beautiful summer day, moving easily on the cinder path circling the calm waters, and I get a tinge of anger and a passing longing. I miss the fact that no matter what I do, no matter how hard I work out or train, I will never jog like I used to or even really jog at all. The way my leg was reattached doesn't provide the muscle support to move my leg so I can jog. I certainly can stride and hop-step, stride, and hop-step as I try to approximate jogging, but all that does is put extra stress on my good right leg and after several minutes, both that and my back hurt and I'm worn out!

The flash of regret or anger passes as quickly as it comes, and I remind myself that losing my leg allowed me to live. The equation **Life > Limb** is as true as it ever was.

CaringBridge Post
January 17, 2013
A leg by any other name
28 days after the surgery

I have been calling my surgically altered left leg my "short leg." But it is much more than the physical result of the surgery. That leg represents that the cancer has been cut out of my body. It is also the foundation I will use for a prosthetic that will allow me to walk again, to jog and to play golf. In short, to live a normal life.

My left leg is my base leg. I will rebuild my ability to move in all manner because I have this leg. It is the necessary antecedent to my recovery.

Instead of looking at the shortened leg with my backward foot as an oddity I am beginning to see it as the first piece of the puzzle that is my recovery. I am learning to celebrate the leg and in time, I hope to celebrate the need for the lack of movement required to make sure my base leg, my foundation leg, heals well and allows me to accept the prosthetic that allows me to walk again.

CaringBridge Post
January 19, 2013
Thirty days
31 days after the surgery

This morning marks 30 days since the morning of December 21. It was at some point early in the morning of the 21st that they wrapped up my surgery and moved me to the ICU. Later the next afternoon they brought me out from the anesthesia, and I was able to see Cindy, Bonnie and my mom.

In many ways the time seems faster than 30 days should and sometimes this feels like it has always been the way it is now. I have certainly come a long way in accepting my new reality and adjusting to the bed rest the doctor requires. After the surgery they told me I would require six months of inactivity for my new hip to fuse. Since then, they told me it may be less time and in the end the X-rays will determine when the bones have fused. If it is six months, I am 1/6 of the way there and if it is shorter the percentage is even larger.

I am getting better at handling the highs and lows that every day brings, and the highs far outweigh the lows. Last night I slept for a total of seven hours, the first time I had seven hours sleep since the operation. I still wake up four hours or so after I start to sleep and need to take some more pain meds, but I am generally able to get back to sleep, at least recently. As my ability to sleep through the night has increased, I've seen a correlation between being well-rested and how my days go. My overall anxiety has lessened and I'm learning to use some of the coping strategies that Cindy's teaching me to knock down the anxiety when it appears. I expect that as I sleep better, learn more, and continue to gain a better understanding of who I am I will feel better each day. One of the struggles I face is that as I feel better, I want to do more, but I can't. I need to be still and that gets tougher as I heal. We go back to Boston on February 1 for another X-ray and to meet with the orthopedic and vascular surgeons. Hopefully, the X-rays show my healing is progressing well.

Cindy and I and my mother want to thank all our friends and family and supporters who have helped us both directly and indirectly. Whether someone is helping us by picking up a prescription or keeping us in their thoughts it means so much to us. The guestbook comments in CaringBridge mean so much to me. I wish I could respond to the comments as I read them, but the site doesn't allow that. Thanks for all the love and support, it sustains me.

CaringBridge Post
January 24, 2013
Undeserved love
36 days after the surgery

This is an essay I wrote for myself a couple of days ago. As I reread it, I realized that I needed to share how much support I have received:

My wife and my mother have dedicated themselves to my well-being. My mother Carlena, at age eighty-one, is here with me all day while Cindy is at work. She gets my meals, she empties my bedside urinal, she brings the medications I need to keep my bowels moving, my blood thin, and my blood pressure low. She picks up and cleans up and sleeps in between her efforts.

When Cindy gets home from work, she takes care of the rest of the house (beyond the four-room apartment that I live in) she does the day's laundry and checks to make sure I am okay. After retreating upstairs to decompress from her job as a clinical therapist for an hour or two, she is back downstairs to talk with me and my mother and get all of us ready for bed.

My sister also belongs on this list. She has changed her working hours too many times to count to accompany me to the surgeons and oncologists, to make trips to Boston and in every instance, she has used her medical training to make sure all the right questions get asked and answered.

This love washes over me like a strong summer wind. It pushes me and I stumble against its force. I am driven to my knees by the strength and example of their love. I am humble. I am unworthy. I have done nothing in my life to be treated with such kindness. It is hard to accept and at times I weep deeply because of the pureness of their intent and effort on my behalf.

This is love. Without any thought except how they can help me, they proceed. When they say, "I love you," their words hammer against my heart with a force I can't express and have never felt before. I must find a way to be able to thank them. But I can't imagine how.

At times I simply fill up with emotions and cry out through tears and labored breath. To receive such simple, pure love is almost painful. I struggle to express the depth of my feelings, my unworthiness, my sadness that their lives now revolve around mine.

They reassure me that it is not a burden and that they could not imagine doing anything else. I am surrounded by angels, by beings with a greater closeness to the power of the universe than I know. They are my support and my heroes. One day, I hope to be half as altruistic and giving as they have been. When that day happens, I will be a blessed human being. In the meantime, I have their example of true love to guide my thoughts and behavior each day. I am becoming a better, deeper, more loving person; more in touch with my emotions, feelings and the knowledge that love is a power unto itself.

Bill Fitzgerald

In response to my *Undeserved love* post my college teammate Bill Fitzgerald replied with a simple post: "YOU are my hero!—Fitz." It was a remarkable and wonderful thing for him to write. What made his response even more meaningful than the sentiments he expressed was how he supported me throughout my entire surgery and recovery.

The story of Fitz and me goes back to when I transferred into Lyndon State College between semesters. Out of the blue I showed up at basketball practice knowing only my old prep school teammate Mike Whaley and the coach—Skip. As I have alluded, I was not a shy presence when it came to basketball. In January of 1981 I was driven by years of feelings of not belonging and fears that I had lost my direction.

In the months prior to that early January arrival, I had stumbled through some of the toughest, darkest, and most shameful periods of my life. In late August of 1980 I had left Maine with my blue 1972 Datsun pickup loaded with everything I owned. I was driving to upstate New York to pick up my longtime girlfriend so we could elope to Vermont. My parents had tried to talk me out of going but by then I was determined to break my father's grip on my life and wouldn't be deterred. We had started dating as freshmen at Castleton State and I was certain that I could be the man she wanted me to be and that we could build our life together.

Once I arrived at her parents' house, we had to overcome their fierce and bitter resistance to our plans before we left in September to drive to Bennington, Vermont, to begin our new life together. We were young and in love and thought we had everything we needed. She had a family heirloom gold ring from her grandmother that we had sized for her wedding band. We found a tiny apartment attached to an old farmhouse outside of town and arranged with the Town Hall to pick up the paperwork for a marriage license. She got a job as a part-time stringer for the local newspaper and I found work as an overnight security guard at a ski area thirty-six miles away. It took me an hour to drive the back roads of Vermont to work each evening. The only thing we didn't have was enough money to do all that needed to be done. We barely had enough money to pay the rent and buy gas and food. Often, we went without food. We tried to save enough money to get our own house in town and begin our life together.

On Thanksgiving we had only oatmeal in the house and no milk, so we had our oatmeal with a little extra water and sugar. Late in the day our landlord invited us over for pie. When we walked into their kitchen the remains of a massive feast were everywhere: turkey, sweet potatoes, stuffing . . . the works . . . everything still out on the counters.

We had a slice of pie, a cup of coffee and returned to our three-room apartment.

At some point in early December, I came to realize that I couldn't get married; I was too young, too uncertain of myself, and too scared. I didn't know what to do. I knew that she was committed to me and that I would be breaking her heart. Beyond that, her family was deeply religious, and they would not accept her back easily.

In the end I bailed out. Just before Christmas Day 1980 we drove to my parents' home and explained that I couldn't marry her as I had promised. She stayed with my parents while I headed north to Lyndonville, Vermont, in late December. Just after New Year's she returned home and enrolled at Plattsburgh State University. We haven't spoken since. I wish more than I can say that I had been better to that sweet young woman. She did not deserve the reality that I thrust upon her.

When I walked into the gym for my first practice with my new team, I was an emotional wreck. Basketball, as it had always been, was my sanctuary. The one place I mostly fit in. However, in this case I was joining a group that had played an entire semester without me and I was ineligible to play in games that spring because of NCAA transfer regulations. I could only practice. Unfortunately, I just did what I always did when it came to basketball and in the end, I didn't make a good first impression. My drive and competitiveness didn't allow me to see that I needed to blend in with the team and relationships that were well-formed before my arrival.

Fitzy and I never really hit it off. We played the same small forward position and he had built his place on the team through diligence and hard work. He had been cut from the team as a freshman despite having been a star player at a small northern Vermont high school. Billy wasn't quick, and he couldn't jump exceedingly high. Skip hadn't seen anything that would lead him to believe that he could help the team. Later in his freshman year when a couple of players left the team, Fitz approached Skip asking if he needed help with practice as there weren't enough players to scrimmage. Skip took him back and Fitz began to show that despite his physical limitations he was a good player who could contribute. In the end he scored over 1,000 points in his career.

That January however, I guarded Fitz many times in practice and I was determined to show Skip what I could do. If I could score on him, I did. If I could make a steal or a block, I did. I was more athletic than he was even if I wasn't as good an all-around player. We battled hard every day on the court and didn't speak too much off the court. As time went on our relationship settled into an acceptance of each other but I would never describe us as close. Even our senior year when Fitz, Mike Whaley, and I were tri-captains we just took care of business on the court and went our separate ways afterwards.

Our relationship began to deepen after college as I grew older and hopefully a bit wiser and when Billy had some difficult family issues that allowed me to see the depth of his character as a man, father, and husband. By the time my cancer diagnosis arrived in 2011 we were more than twenty-five years removed from our playing days and saw each other at the Turkey Bowl, a touch football game we all played in each year and several times at get-togethers in northern Vermont.

When I was diagnosed with cancer, I wasn't the first of our college cohort to have cancer. Several of us had suffered through cancer and come out the other side. In every case, those affected and our group had been concerned and even scared, but we had all come through it. However, when my cancer returned and the decision was made to amputate my leg it took things to a different level for my friends who were all ex-college athletes. Losing a leg was different.

Cindy and I had started the CaringBridge site to help her by setting up a place for updates on my condition during and after my amputation, so she didn't have to make dozens of phone calls. Once he learned of the CaringBridge site Fitz had been a constant presence. Every time I posted he had a reply. His comments ran the gamut from "Keep up the good work" . . . "What a great attitude" . . . "Look forward to covering you in the next Turkey Bowl" with his tongue firmly in his cheek . . . to the "YOU are my hero!" post on January 25.

Months later, when we had a party to celebrate and thank all the friends and family who had helped up so much, I asked Bill about his faithful postings. He told me, "When I heard about what was happening to you, I didn't know what to say so I just decided that I would post something positive every time you posted." He did just that and it made such a difference.

Dependency

As I had learned to make my way in the world, I had become extremely independent. This was a result of my emotional shortcomings and my need to remain in control. I used to joke for years that I could be left alone in a new town with one hundred dollars in my pocket and I would be okay because I can take care of myself! I would find a way to make a new life wherever you dropped me.

Of course, having cancer and losing my leg disabused me of all pretense when it came to strength and capability. I wrote a post about my independence.

CaringBridge Post
January 29, 2013
Dependency
39 days after the surgery

Back on January 21 Joe Melnick, a longtime professional and personal friend wrote in my guestbook about the difficult way I have had to "develop my dependency."

Since then, I have thought about his statement and talked it over with Cindy. I was, by nature and nurture, a very independent person. I had grown into a man who emotionally did not know how to and did not think I needed to rely on others. In fact, it was scary to think about being in a situation where I was dependent. My independence was a badge of honor for me. I knew, and said, that I would always be okay if I found myself alone. I saw myself as resilient, strong, and able to care for myself. Obviously, I was wrong.

As I have made my way through my cancer diagnosis and the surgeries that culminated with my December 20th amputation, I have had to face the fact that not only do I need others to help me physically through this long rehab process but, more importantly, I now realize how much I need others to emotionally support me as I make my way through this new reality.

The deepest realization has been how liberating it is to allow others to help and how much more connected I feel with the world around me as others express their emotions in actions and words. I have come to realize that dependency is not weakness but strength. It is like the difference in durability between a strand of string and a thick braided rope. While both are made of the same material, the braided rope will withstand hundreds and thousands of times the stress of the string. I have gone from being a piece of string to part of an extraordinarily strong rope.

This is all part of a much larger and longer journey for me. My life has been changed forever in many ways. Some of the changes are obvious like my leg while others are hidden but even more potent and transformative in my life. Learning of, and welcoming my dependency has been life altering.

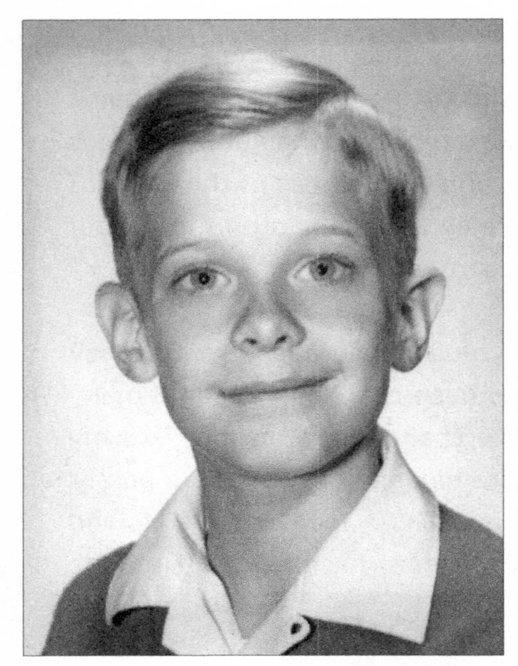

5th Grade
Me the summer we moved back to Maine.

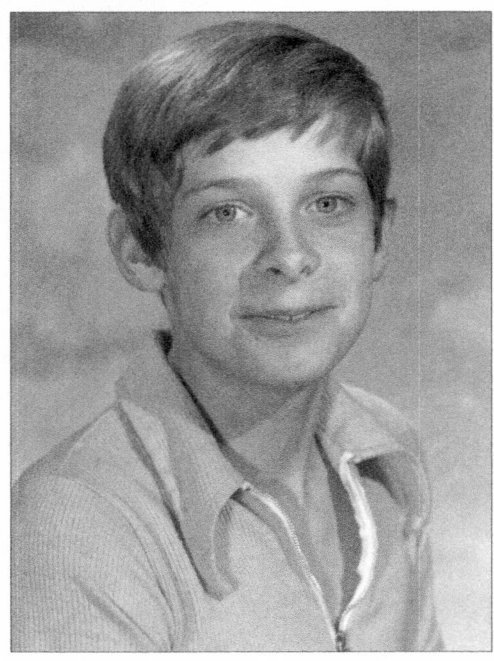

8th Grade
When I began to work at basketball.

My senior year of high school—1977.

Left: A breakaway layup at Maine Central Institute in 1978.

Below: Shooting a free throw outdoors at age twenty.

Scoring on the baseline. Note all five defenders are in the area.

Blocking a shot. Mike Whaley (#25) tried to take the charge before the shot.

Above: Working with post players at Keene State College in fall 1988.

Left: On the sidelines versus the University of New Haven in 1989.

A note I sent to Dr. Lisa Rutstein after finishing a 10K in July 2012 following the earlier surgeries to cut out the cancer.

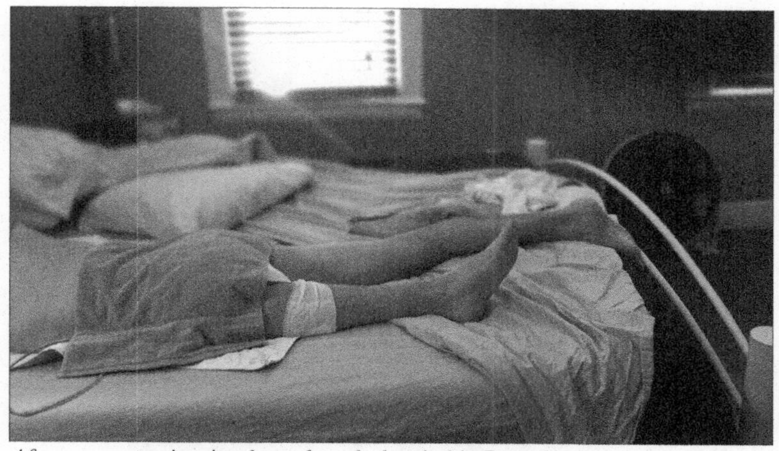

After my amputation, just home from the hospital in December 2012. Still bandaged from surgery.

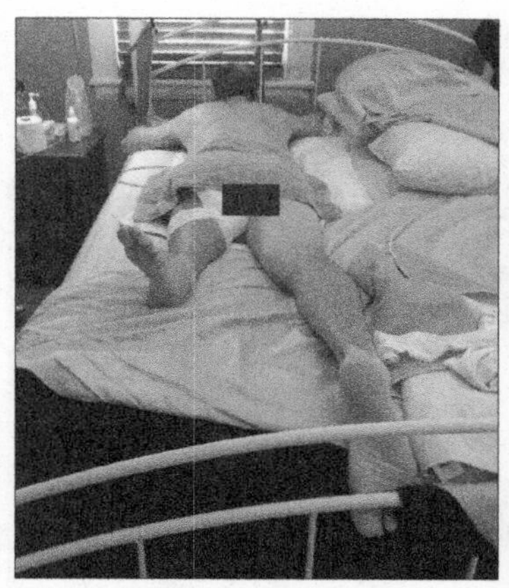

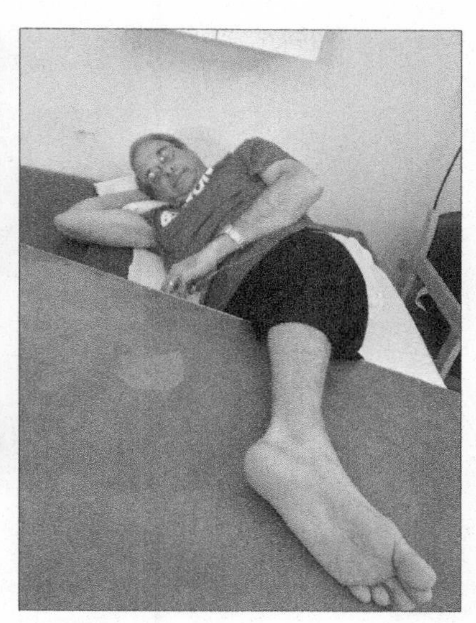

Above: A different view after my amputation.December 2012.

Right: Receiving electric stimulation to help muscle development in physical therapy. May 2013.

First day playing golf on my new leg. One day before getting the official clearance to stand on the leg. June 19, 2013.

After my hole in one. September 2013.

Hitting to the green from 130 yards at the Samoset in 2017. I made this shot for an eagle.

Lining up a putt in the Gorham Savings Bank Maine Amputee Open in 2018.

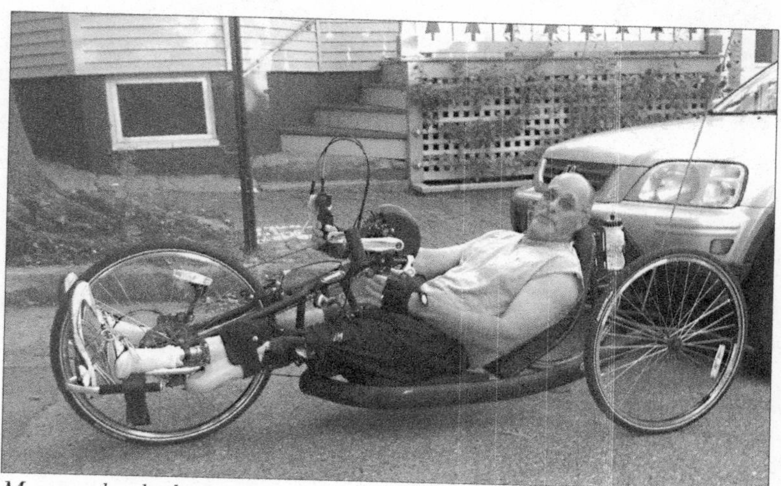

Me on my handcycle.

My favorite picture of Cindy. Taken in an outdoor café in Savannah, Georgia.

Cindy

One of the deepest and most personal understandings that came from my cancer surgeries, the amputation and my rehabilitation was how much my wife Cindy loved me. Her dedication, effort, and support were critical to me coming out the other side of some very dark moments.

CaringBridge Post
January 30, 2013
Cindy
40 days after the surgery

For some time now I have been searching for the right words to describe my wonderful wife, Cindy, and how foundational she has been in my life. I use the term foundational because she is the foundation, the very thing that supports all I am, of my life.

I have written about Cindy, my mom, and my

sister as angels, "beings with a greater closeness to the power of the universe than I know." Yet there are great differences between sister, mother, and wife.

My sister, in our case, came home from the hospital to find two big brothers waiting for her. She had to adapt to the family she was born into and has grown to be a wonderful woman who has been a great support to me in many ways. A mother receives the gift of a child with all the responsibility to grow that young life to adulthood. Even now my mother tells her friends that I am still her "baby" at age fifty-three.

A wife is different. She makes a choice as an adult to completely join her life with that of another. The decision, the commitment, is life-changing.

Cindy has changed my life profoundly. I am a much more complete man because she is in my life. She lives a life filled with empathy for others, her intentions are pure, and they are always designed to lift up the people around her. Cindy is incredibly focused on others and I am the recipient of her efforts more than anyone else on earth. She loves me unconditionally and she has taught me what unconditional love really is.

I read once that the secret to a good marriage

was falling in love with the same person over and over again. Well, by that definition I have a great marriage because I find more things to love about Cindy on a daily basis. Her love for me is unyielding. Her ability to cope with the pressures that have been heaped upon us in the past year and a half as we have battled cancer and in the years prior as she cared for her mother during her last days is immense. She is a warrior for those that she loves, and I thank God she loves me.

When I was first diagnosed with myxofibrosarcoma Cindy was just beginning a highly competitive and very intense one-year, advanced-standing master of social work program. We discussed her switching to the normal two-year track, but she decided, rightly, that she could complete the program. And she did, with distinction, the same way she finished her undergraduate degree. Summa Cum Laude. Her ability to complete her MSW in just one year, while always being there to support me is just another indication of her drive, compassion, and ability to focus. She will tell you that completing the program was incredibly stressful, and it was. So was caring for an outgoing, headstrong husband who had just been diagnosed with cancer and who would have four operations in the first five months of her master's work. Yet she did both with grace and her always present gentle spirit.

> I mentioned at the beginning of this essay that I have been searching for the right words to describe what Cindy means to me. That is because words fail me when I try to translate the emotions I feel into language others might understand. I love her beyond words. I strive every day to demonstrate how happy I am that she chose me. I only hope my actions will suffice when words fail.

It has been eight years since I wrote those words, and they are truer today than ever. We have been married for twenty-four years and together for twenty-six, and Cindy's ability to understand me and support me is an ever-present gift. I like to think that I do a better job for her given the things I have learned about myself in the time that has elapsed since my surgery. As time goes on, I am privileged to live with a woman who faces each day resolutely. She is introspective and a continuous learner, always looking at what she may do to make our world a better place. If angels walk among us, they look like her.

Magda Abdou

During my diagnosis and fight with cancer I have had the tremendous good fortune to have outstanding medical professionals working on my behalf. Not only were these people professionals but to a person they were caring and thoughtful individuals. I have mentioned Dr. Ferrone, the orthopedist who led my rotationplasty surgery. I should also mention Dr. Menard the lead vascular surgeon, Dr. Butrynski, the oncologist at Dana Farber who took such an interest in me, Dr. Evans my oncologist in Maine and Dr. Lisa Rutstein, who was my surgeon through my surgeries leading up to my amputation. Lisa was a true pro who worked with me every step of the way to get me the best outcome even as the cancer returned and we headed to Brigham and Women's for the rotationplasty.

One of the best professionals I encountered on this journey was not practicing as a doctor when I met her but what she did allowed everything else to happen. I wrote the following post about her.

CaringBridge Post
February 1, 2013
Boston and Magda Abdou
42 days after the surgery

Bonnie and I returned from our trip to Brigham & Women's earlier this afternoon. We had a good drive on a beautiful day.

I had an ultrasound on my left leg to check the condition of my arteries and veins as well as a series of X-rays on my reconstructed left hip to check on the position and fusing of the joint. The ultrasound showed that the circulation in my leg is in great shape as the senior vascular technologist and the cardiologist on duty took turns looking at the vessels and in particular the anastomosis (my word of the day). It refers to the surgical joining of two blood vessels of the major arteries and veins. The X-rays were completed but I was unable to meet with Dr. Ferrone as he was called into surgery. I did look at the X-rays myself and while they looked good to me, as Cindy pointed out when I texted her, it is probably important to have someone who did go to medical school weigh in on how they look. Dr. Ferrone will call me next week to discuss the X-rays.

When I arrived for my ultrasound, I found Magda Abdou waiting with my file in her hand. I had first met Magda more than two months ago when she did the preoperative ultrasound that the vascular surgeon, Dr. Menard, used as his guide for the surgery. When we met for my pre-op ultrasound Magda had told me that Dr. Menard often requested that she complete the ultrasound on his complicated surgeries. When she told me her background I understood why.

Magda had emigrated to the US from Egypt where she had practiced for twenty-three years as an OB/GYN surgeon. However, because when she emigrated her medical degree was more than ten years old, she would have had to repeat her residency; a three-year commitment in order to practice as a physician in the US. With teenage children to raise and college costs looming on the horizon she decided that working as an ultrasound technician was the best and quickest way to help her family in their new country and she threw herself into becoming the best technician she could be. As I watched and listened to Magda and the cardiologist discuss my ultrasound this morning it was obvious she had succeeded as the two discussed my case as peers, each asking the other if they agreed with the other's interpretations. It was very reassuring to see her again and to have her involved in my care. The vascular surgeon's office told me they will be doing an ultrasound of my left leg every three months for the next fifteen months so I will probably see Magda again in May.

I did see Magda on my next trip and several trips thereafter. She was a reassuring presence as I recovered from my life-altering surgery. On one of my last trips I asked her about her children, whose future she was protecting when she decided to do ultrasound versus returning to school to continue as a surgeon. My recollection is that she has one child who is a dentist, one who is a doctor, and one who became a CPA.

So It Is

CaringBridge Post
February 4, 2013
My left foot (sounds like a movie doesn't it?)
46 days after the surgery

I was reading tonight when my left foot began to itch. I somewhat absentmindedly reached down to scratch the itch and there, about where my knee ought to be, was my foot. As I held my foot in my hand and rubbed my heel it was the strangest sensation. It is not as though I don't realize every day that my leg is different, and I am certainly very careful as I maneuver around the apartment. But there it was, my foot, facing backward, itching. It was my foot, it felt like my foot and looked like my foot, but it was in the wrong place. I just rubbed it and took a deep breath and reminded myself that the cancer is gone and soon enough I will be learning to walk on a prosthetic attached to that uniquely placed foot.

One of the books I read after my surgery was *Black Elk Speaks*, written in 1932 by John G. Neihardt. The book is the story of Black Elk, an Oglala Lakota medicine man. Neihardt interviewed Black Elk who spoke in the Lakota language. Black Elk's son, Ben Black Elk, who was present at the interviews, translated his father's words into English. There was much to learn from the words of the elderly medicine man. One of the things I took away was the Lakota phrase *hetchetu aloh* (phonetically het'che'tu' ye'lo). The phrase means "so it is." After my surgery, *hetchetu aloh*. I see my life and actions from this point forward. My new reality, while different from before is simply the world as it is.

Marcus Aurelius, the Roman emperor and stoic philosopher wrote, "Think of the life you have lived until now as over and, as a dead man, see what's left as a bonus and live it according to nature. Love the hand that fate deals you and play it as your own, for what could be more fitting."

Today is all we are promised, and we need to live it as we find it.

Coaching

In my nine years as a college basketball coach I was fortunate to work with some excellent coaches and coach players who tried their best to perform. While completing my master's degree at Indiana University I was able to attend many practices of the 1984 Olympic team as they prepared in Assembly Hall in Bloomington before leaving for Los Angeles. I had taken a graduate class in advanced theory of basketball with Bob Knight's assistant coaches Royce Waltman and Kohn Smith (both of whom went on to be fine college head coaches). When the class ended, at about the same time Olympic tryouts began, I asked if I could sit in the press row in Assembly Hall to watch the Olympic practices. Coach Knight said that if I stayed out of the way I was welcome. It was a master class of the first degree. The players (Michael Jordan, Patrick Ewing, Chris Mullin, Sam Perkins, Wayman Tisdale, and Indiana sophomore Steve Alford, among others) on that team went on to win gold in L.A. and became among the best players the world has ever known. While Coach Knight has a rightly deserved reputation as a difficult personality, he was an outstanding teacher of basketball and between the graduate class and the Olympic practices, I saw his theory put into action repeatedly.

But Knight and the Olympic team were not the most important thing to happen at IU regarding my coaching career. Dr. Maryalice Jeremiah was the women's basketball coach at Indiana and she gave me my big break. She allowed me to become a volunteer assistant on her 1984–1985 team. My role was limited to watching early morning conditioning sessions in the fall and practices throughout the winter while I reported back to the coaching staff with any thoughts I had about the players as individuals and the team. I don't think I did much actual hands-on coaching except for helping with the odd drill now and then. I was incredibly surprised when I was called to the basketball office in the early spring of 1985 and told I had an interview for an assistant women's basketball coach position at Kent State. The Indiana staff had set up the interview and I got my first full-time coaching job at age twenty-five. That position led to one year as an assistant women's coach at the University of Pittsburgh before I was offered the job as head women's basketball coach at Division II Keene State College the summer I turned twenty-eight.

At KSC I was fortunate to find a team that was hungry for success. After going 11–15 and graduating the school's all-time leading scorer the year prior, the women on that team, including four talented freshman and no seniors, met the challenge I laid out for them. I was finishing my recruiting duties at Pitt early in the fall so I split time between Pittsburgh and New Hampshire. I was fortunate I had a focused and talented graduate assistant coach, Tim Rapant, who worked with the players through our preseason conditioning when I was absent.

That team set a school record for wins (twenty-one), led the nation in three-point field goals made per game, and won the first ECAC Championship in program history. As a result of the team's play, I was named Coach of the Year in the New England Collegiate Conference. The next year we added two recruits: one who would set the single-game scoring record in the program and the other who would become the school's all-time leading scorer. That team repeated as ECAC Champions, setting another school record for wins.

From Keene State I accepted a position starting a Division III men's program from scratch at a formerly all-women's school. Colby-Sawyer College had decided that coeducation was the only way to save an institution that had served women for generations and hired me to help with that process. I spent a year recruiting and a year later took the court with fifteen freshmen on the roster playing a varsity Division III schedule. As eighteen-year-old boys, that team also rose to the formidable challenge of playing against grown men. They finished that first season 13–12. Against truly long odds they persevered. Night in and night out they left everything they had on the floor and as a result they performed better than anyone could have expected.

Unfortunately, my athletic director, who attended Colby-Sawyer as a student and returned to a coaching and administrative role, had never seen male coaches interacting with male athletes and she thought I was too tough on those young men. I tried to explain to her that I had been tougher and demanded more consistency from my Division II women who were on scholarship than on those eighteen-year-old boys, but in the end, after a lost season the next year, I resigned. My last year at Colby-Sawyer was the only time I was not satisfied with my own effort. I tried to coach in a way that was not true to myself and I didn't give that team the opportunity they deserved. In the end, after a year as an assistant at the University of Southern Maine in 1993, I left coaching as a full-time profession.

For the last fifteen years I have worked in a very part-time role helping Matt Richards, one of my former players, with his community college team. I occasionally go to practice, watch tape of opponents to help develop game strategies, discuss special situations with Matt and his assistants, and attend home games as an extra set of eyes on the bench.

I hope I gave back as much as I got from the men and women I had the opportunity to coach.

Matt Richards

On February 6 I talked with Dr. Ferrone by telephone and he told me that my X-rays looked excellent and that he was pleased with the progress my fused hip/femur was showing; the bones were showing positive signs of fusing together. He said that while I still needed to lie down for twenty-two to twenty-three hours a day, I could switch from a walker to crutches, begin to do core, isometric exercises, go for a weekly car ride (lying prone) to get out of the house, and if I stayed prone, I could go out to events. The next night I went to a basketball game.

CaringBridge Post
February 7, 2013
More than a game
49 days after the surgery

After getting permission from Dr. Ferrone, I attended the Southern Maine Community College versus Central Maine Community College basketball game at SMCC. One of my former players Matt Richards is the athletic director and men's basketball coach at SMCC. Matt played his freshman year for me at Colby-Sawyer College and we have stayed close since then. During Matt's ten years at SMCC, at his request, I have made time to watch the occasional practice and talk to his teams a couple of times a year. In the last two years, after my initial diagnosis with cancer, I made a commitment to Matt and the program to make two or three practices a week and attend all home games as a volunteer assistant coach. I had not been to SMCC since a couple of days prior to my December 20th surgery.

I called Matt to tell him I could come to the game and after first confirming that Cindy was at least aware of my plan to attend the game if not 100 percent in agreement, Matt said he would take care of all the details. He called me back to tell me that I would be able to park immediately beside an emergency door and that he would arrange to have the parking space reserved and the door open so I could get inside without having to walk too far. I asked Steve Jordan to drive me to the game and sit with me behind the team bench. We put my mesh chaise lounge into his car and headed to South Portland.

I should have known something was up when we

pulled into the parking lot and there was one security guard waiting outside to move the orange cones that reserved the parking space and another guard just inside the emergency door to let us in. Matt met us at the door and helped Steve and me set up my reclined chaise lounge for me and a padded chair from the team bench for Steve. As we came into the gymnasium the women's team was just starting the second half of their game and I looked around to find the men's team who should have been right there watching the women and waiting to go into their locker room for their pregame instructions. But the players were nowhere to be found. Matt had taken them to another room and had not told them I was coming. He brought them back into the gym once I was settled and I had a long line of players welcome me with hugs and congratulations on my successful surgery.

It was great to see and talk with the players I had grown so close to before I had to leave for my surgery. There is a unique bond that can occur when you are working hard with someone to help them maximize their potential. Over the course of the preseason and early season, several of the players and I had had open and honest discussions about their strengths and weaknesses on the basketball court as well as their goals in life and I felt that perhaps I had been able to help some of them realize that they had a greater future than they had imagined for themselves. People often see coaches on the sidelines being very demonstrative with their players and wonder what all the emotion is about. In truth, the relationship that allows that emotional interplay is built during hours of practice and the trust that is developed between player and coach. On a good team the players know that the coach wants what is best for each player and the team.

There was a bit of melancholy because two of the players I enjoyed working with the most were no longer with the team. One made some bad off-the-court decisions and had to leave school and the other had decided he wasn't happy continuing to play and had left the team. Both young men remain good guys, I hope they figure out what they want out of life and find the most direct path to a successful future.

But it turned out that the current players were only the first part of the night for me. After they had greeted me, I had several of the alumni who had played for Matt over the last ten years stop by to tell me how happy they were to see me out and about. They were followed by the TV crew, the stat crew, the opposing coaches and many, many other friends of the program. I had so many people stopping to see me that I really was not able to watch the women's game. Feeling lucky to be a part of the SMCC program, I followed the men's team into the locker room for Matt's pregame talk.

As we came out of the locker room for the men's pregame warm-ups, I settled back into my reclining chair ready to watch a hard-fought game between Southern Maine and their intrastate rival Central Maine and maybe help Matt with some insight I might see (I was, after all, there as an assistant coach). But Matt wasn't done yet. The introductions of the players included a light show worthy of an NBA game and once the players were introduced the PA announcer introduced the coaching staff, saving my name for last. Matt had written a special introduction for me. The PA announcer said, among other things, that I was a mentor to Matt and back with the program after a successful surgery, having beaten cancer. The crowd, having been whipped into a frenzy by the light show, the music, and the announcer's delivery of my introduction gave me a standing ovation. It was very humbling.

I went to the game to see the players and the coaches and watch a good game. I got so much more.

It was the hard-fought contest I thought it would be. Injuries left Southern Maine with only nine players dressed for the game and one of those was playing for the first time in a month as he recovered from a badly sprained ankle. SMCC outscored CMCC by six in the first half but couldn't match the other team's depth and ended up losing by eight.

After the game, the opposing players all filed by to shake my hand (and Steve's as he sat beside me). But once again, there was another and most important moment to come. After the crowd had filed out of the gym and Steve and I had talked with several more supporters of the team who came over to say hello to me, we were making our way to the door when the starting center for CMCC asked if he could talk with me. As the tall young man came over to us, I wasn't sure what to expect. I had shaken his hand with his teammates after the game and I didn't know what he wanted now. He shook my hand again and said, "I just wanted to tell you what an inspiration you are to me. I lost my grandmother to cancer. I don't know if you noticed but I wrote her date of birth and date of death on my game shoes. I play every game for her. The fact that you have been able to beat cancer inspires me and I just wanted you to know."

I thanked him and told him what a fine young man he was. He shook my hand again and was gone.

That private moment was far more touching and humbling than all the greetings and hugs and the ovation earlier in the night.

The next day I texted Steve to thank him for driving me to South Portland. He texted back that he had enjoyed the game and that watching me be greeted and talk with so many people all night long had a profound effect on him. As he said in his text, "It is only at their funerals that most people first learn of the impact one has made upon the lives of others. Last evening, I got to observe a man who clearly has made an impact on the lives of many people, be acknowledged by them personally, when he was very much alive! It was a moving experience for me."

It was a moving and educational experience for me. Cancer has been a strange companion these last months and years. Do I wish that I never had cancer, that I still had my leg, intact with all the muscles that were cut out earlier? Of course I do. However, the personal growth I have experienced and the deep understanding of me and my life that has come as a result of all I have gone through are not a gift I wish to give back.

Home Work

The day after the SMCC game the eastern half of the US was hit by a "bomb cyclone"—a nor'easter blizzard that formed from the combination of two areas of low pressure joining to form an extratropical cyclone with winds of 102 miles per hour (164 km/h) in Nova Scotia and 89 mph (143 km/h) in Maine and record snowfall throughout the Northeast. Portland received a record 31.9 inches (81 cm.) while parts of Connecticut reached 40 inches (100 cm).

At our house we were immobilized for days. After the storm, on the beautiful still, sunny day that followed, I remember looking out my window as Cindy, all four-foot-eleven-inches of her, shoveled a path from our front door to the street. All I could see was the snow flying as she threw it high over her head and out of the six-foot deep drift that was our yard. The snow was over the lower half of our first-floor windows and we hunkered down while all about us the city slowly, over days, returned to normal. The snow did little to relieve me of the anxiety that my inactivity sometimes brought on.

CaringBridge Post
February 20, 2013
Mom
62 days after the surgery

On Friday February 15th I came to the realization that after more than 60 straight days with Cindy and me in Maine, Boston, and back in Maine, my mother could go back to her home in Brunswick, Maine. I was finally strong enough and confident enough to be home during the day, while Cindy was at work, on my own. The last piece of the puzzle was figuring out how I could navigate the kitchen on crutches while preparing simple meals. I thought that if I used a carpenter's apron I could go to the refrigerator, place my food and condiments in the apron and go across the kitchen on my crutches to the counter or stove to prepare my meals. Steve Jordan was kind enough to get the carpenters apron and after a quick test I realized I could fend for myself in the kitchen.

My mother had accompanied us on the train to Boston for my operation; she and Cindy shared a hotel room for nine days and took turns supporting each other through my longer-than-expected surgery and my initial recovery in the hospital. It has only been recently that I realized two things about my time in the hospital: 1) I was pretty heavily medicated, and 2) My memory of those nine days is pretty hazy. But my mom was there providing whatever support she could to me or Cindy, 24 hours a day.

When we returned to Maine on December 28th, she moved in with us. At first, she and Cindy shared duties and took turns taking care of me in my weakened state. Then, as I became marginally stronger and Cindy was able to return to work, my mother became my chief caretaker during the day. She brought me my medications, emptied my bedside urinal, fixed my meals, and brought them to me in bed, kept the kitchen and bathroom clean and generally did everything and anything that I needed to make my life more comfortable. She was on call 24 hours a day. At age 81, she slept at first on a cot and then eventually on a more comfortable daybed. Even the daybed was not a real bed, with a real mattress. Yet, there was no complaint and when I told her that I thought she was doing too much, pushing herself too hard, she explained to me that as my mother she couldn't imagine being anywhere else when I had such a great need. She was truly selfless.

Love is an imperfect thing. There is no right or wrong way to love yet we all have expectations of those around us who love us. I know that if I reflect back on my childhood there are things that I wish had been different; times I wish my mother and father had more time for me and I suspect that most of us can think of things our parents should have done differently. But I experienced a rare gift with my mother. I was able to, as an adult who now understands the pressures and worries of life, watch my mother express her love through her actions, day after day, week after week, tedious task after tedious task. She was everything I could ever hope a mother to be and her love was perfect for me.

CaringBridge Post
March 3, 2013
Two weeks on my own
73 days after the surgery

It has been two weeks since my mother went home after more than two months living with Cindy and me and helping both of us in more ways than we can name. When I woke up on that Sunday morning 14 days ago, I was uncertain as to how I would be able to adapt to my newfound independence. I am happy to report that it has been a wonderful success.

I have had to discover new adaptations in the

way I do things to accomplish some of the normal everyday things in a household. For example, after washing the dishes I must move them one at a time down the counter from the sink to the cupboard. That means moving all the dishes three feet and then moving myself before I move them all again an additional three feet to where they need to be put away. Where before I would have stacked up all the dishes, carried them over and put them away in two minutes; it now takes five minutes, but it gets done.

The changes one makes in everyday routines to cope with a handicap at first seem burdensome and I am sure to an outsider looking in they are. But when you live with the disability and you find a way to take care of yourself, even with a repetitive routine like putting away the dishes, it comes with a sense of pride.

The other skill I am developing is patience. Patience with myself, my situation, and with others. Cindy will tell you that I always did things fast—the quicker I got something done the sooner I could move to the next thing. Now I have a different perspective. I go through my daily life much more interested in quality than quantity. Part of the change is based on my increased awareness of my own vulnerability; if I slip and fall on this rebuilt hip, I may forfeit my chance for a prosthetic. I now go slow because it is the right thing to do physically. Surprisingly, I find myself being more methodical mentally as well. I now will often take the time to read an entire research article whereas before I would have just skimmed it and paid attention to the abstract and/or charts and graphs. This is just another way my life has become richer for having to deal with the cancer and the aftermath of the surgery.

I am more independent than I was several weeks ago, I take care of myself during the day and try to have a meal prepared when Cindy gets home from work, but I am not the same person I was before the surgery. That person is gone. Now, in so many ways I see life differently and it seems, more clearly than before.

Friends

CaringBridge Post
March 19, 2013
Tests and other updates
90 days after the surgery

Even though the doctors believe my surgery to be curative I will need continued testing for at least the next five years and to that end I had an MRI last Friday and a CT scan this past Monday. I don't like MRIs for two reasons: first, I don't like small spaces and anyone who has had an MRI knows they feel confining; and secondly, it is sometimes hard to stay perfectly still for the entire test. The latter was the problem on Friday. But it wasn't my fault.

In the past an MRI of my leg lasted about 45 minutes. This time I was in the tube for almost three hours as the techs had to reset the machine three times and inject dye to get the views that the surgeon had requested. I had taken a Valium to help with the claustrophobia, and the time went as fast as three hours can, but I felt bad for Steve Jordan who had driven me to the appointment. He had brought work to do but by the time I came out to the waiting room he had used up the batteries of his laptop and his iPad.

Steve has been a solid support for Cindy and me ever since I have come home from the hospital and he played a huge part in getting our downstairs apartment ready for my return. Since we have been home, he has often just shown up after a snowstorm (like he did yesterday and this morning) to shovel our driveway and our walkway. He and Deb are more like family than friends.

On Monday my friend and golf buddy Drew Juris drove me to my CT scan. It was much less eventful than Friday's MRI and I was out in 30 or 40 minutes. I don't really mind CT Scans. They are relatively quick and the contrast solution they inject doesn't give me a burning sensation like it does to some people—just a gentle warmth that spreads from my head down to my chest and abdomen. We stopped at Dunkin' Donuts because

I had not been able to eat before the CT scan, and picked up some breakfast on the way home.

I had started Monday the same way I do each Monday, Wednesday, and Friday. Bruce, my running partner before my surgery, comes over at 7:30 a.m. and we lift weights. Of course I can't do anything that involves my rebuilt hip, but we have a solid routine that works our arms, chests, shoulders, and abs. Using bands and dumbbells I can work out on my bed and Bruce does his work in a chair and on the floor. Back in the late fall when the tumor in my leg was growing so big that I couldn't run without considerable pain I told Bruce that soon I would not be able to run in the mornings anymore. His response was, "That's okay, if we can't run, we'll walk and if you can't walk, we'll have coffee." After I came home from the hospital Bruce did bring coffee in the mornings before I was stable enough to begin lifting.

Steve, Drew, and Bruce are emblematic of the tremendous support I have received and continue to receive as I make my way through this journey. When I stop to think of the people who do things, big and small, to help Cindy and me I realize how lucky we are.

I am writing this book in the late fall of 2020, almost

eight years since my surgery, and I say again how lucky I am to have the friends I do. I am truly blessed.

CaringBridge Post
March 30, 2013
Medicine and friends
101 days after the surgery

Ray Geremia taught journalism and was the faculty advisor to our college newspaper. He was an excellent newspaperman, a former editor at the *Washington Post* and before that, a reporter for newspapers and wire services and went all over the world during his career. He taught me many things, but the biggest lesson I remember was to never bury the lead. Put the important stuff first! So: I can now go outside; I can drive; and I can go to work (all on a limited basis).

Over the last two weeks I had an MRI and a CT scan and on Friday, Bonnie and I went to Boston for X-rays and to meet with the surgeon and my oncologist. The MRI and the CT scan came back fine. No sign of cancer! I will have another set of tests in three months. The X-rays showed that I am growing bone around my rebuilt hip and Dr. Ferrone said that I can begin to return to a normal schedule while we wait for the hip to continue its healing. He was clear that I can't push too hard but at the same time I can do whatever is comfortable apart from putting any weight on my left leg. It was tremendous news.

On the way home from Boston, we had an appointment with the prosthetist who will be designing and building my artificial leg. I had asked Dr. Ferrone if we could get started with that work while my hip was still healing so that when the hip was ready, I would be very close to having a new leg versus having to wait several months to have one designed and built. The meeting with the prosthetist went very well and we decided that I will do a month of physical therapy to develop some of the reattached muscles in my left leg and to increase the flexibility of my left foot and ankle. In early May we will begin the formal fitting and design process. I have another X-ray scheduled for June 21. If that looks good, and we have every expectation it will, then I will be able to bear weight on my leg and I will have an artificial leg waiting for me. Friday was a beautiful spring day and it certainly felt like spring to me.

That's the medical news. The *friends* part of my title refers to Steve White. He met me at Dana Farber when we arrived and spent the entire morning with me. Steve and I attended the same college (although not at the same time—he takes great joy in reminding me that he is younger than I am) and we have become friends and business associates through mutual friends over the years. Steve owns a business in Greater Boston and took Friday off to spend the day with me. He has been through a lot in his own family recently and I think it was beneficial to both of us to spend that time together. He is a wonderful man, a good husband and father (who is very proud of his kids and rightly so), a good businessman, and a very good friend. He waited for me when I went in for my X-rays and through my doctor's appointment. We talked before and between appointments, and then went to lunch with Bonnie after we were done at Dana Farber. It was great to see him.

Before I close, I want to take a moment to sincerely thank everyone who has posted responses to my posts. This site is not set up to be interactive, but I want everyone to know how much it means to hear from all of you. At times some of your responses have moved me to laughter and at other times to tears. The community of friends and family that I have in my life has sustained me through this ordeal and continues to sustain me now. Thank you and Happy Easter.

The Dunk That Never Was

CaringBridge Post
April 5, 2013
Mike Whaley's Column
107 days after the surgery

My longtime (since 1977) friend and teammate Mike Whaley is the sports editor for the *Foster's Daily Democrat* family of newspapers. He wrote the column below for this weekend's newspapers. What he doesn't say in his column is that he was thinking of this same play the morning of my surgery. We were separated by 100 miles and 30 years but both of us were reliving a shared moment in time.

Mike's article is reprinted on the following pages.

Loss, Courage and One Smoking Dunk

by Mike Whaley

Foster's Daily Democrat

Saturday, April 6, 2013

It is one of those images in sport that time cannot erode. It is Carlton Fisk gyrating up the first-base line, willing his home run in Game 6 of the 1975 World Series to go fair. It is the United States hockey team storming the ice after upsetting Russia in the 1980 Winter Olympics.

This one is intensely personal, even more so given the circumstances of the last two years.

The play unfolded on a basketball court at Lyndon State College in Northern Vermont 30 years ago. The play was inconsequential. It did not win or lose a game. It did not change momentum. In fact, it didn't even count.

I remember driving to the hoop after a steal, alone and approaching the left side of the basket. As I rise to lay the ball in with my right hand, I suddenly realize, too late, that I have short-armed the shot and it's not going in.

It touches the glass and hangs briefly on the left side of the rim. As it starts to come off, my friend and teammate John LeMieux—all 6-foot-2 of him—alertly following the play, perfectly times his leap, grabs the ball and with two hands dunks it through the basket—a highlight reel play that remains crystal clear 30 years later.

It all happens in the blink of an eye, two- or three-seconds tops, and it doesn't count because the referee waves it off for offensive goaltending.

John, now 53, was thinking of that dunk on Dec. 20 as he was being wheeled into surgery at Dana-Farber Cancer Institute. He was having his left leg removed above the knee to battle a particularly ugly and rare strain of cancer called myxofibrosarcoma.

"It was probably the most athletic, responsive thing I have ever done," he said. "It just happened. Something made me run and (the ball) came into both hands and I was able to go after it. . . . It's bittersweet being 52 or 53, I am long way from doing that, and the leg I jumped off was going."

John spent 20 hours in surgery and another eight days at Dana-Farber, but the procedure was a success. Now he gets around pretty well, waiting for the bones to fuse so that the leg can be fitted later this year with a prosthetic.

Although today John is a financial advisor in Portland, Maine, his passion for basketball never diminished. He was a college coach after Lyndon for nine years, coaching women at Indiana University, Kent State University, Pittsburgh, and Keene State. He was the head coach at KSC, guiding them to a pair of 20-win seasons and two ECAC titles.

Before changing careers, his final coaching stints

were at Colby-Sawyer College as that school's first men's head coach for three years, and then one year as an assistant at the University of Southern Maine in the early 1990s.

John recently got back into coaching as a part-time assistant at Southern Maine Community College in South Portland, a team coached by Matt Richards, a former player of his at Colby-Sawyer.

John's first bout with cancer came two years ago, leading to surgery on his leg that removed cancerous tissue, leaving a chunk of his leg missing that looked like a shark bite.

Before the surgery, John felt he had to tell the SMCC team. He had some fun doing it, telling a story from his Colby-Sawyer days.

Back then, the team was returning to the school after an off-campus practice. During that practice, John had stopped the action and said, "When I'm talking it behooves you to pay attention to me." One player loved the word "behooves."

On the way back to campus, he pipes up from the back of the van, "Hey, coach, teach us a new word."

After this anecdote, John turned to the SMCC players and said, "Now I'm going to teach you a new word," and he wrote myxofibrosarcoma on the blackboard.

"Does anybody know what this is?" John asked.

They all said no.

"It's the cancer I have in my leg," he responded.

It was one of those cancer types that can come

back and it did. He started experiencing stiffness in the spring of 2012 and pain in the leg, so he returned to his Maine doctors on October 12 and an MRI showed a cancerous mass in the leg.

Maine Medical Center said there was not enough tissue left in the leg to remove the cancer and that the entire leg would have to be removed. Dana-Farber offered an alternative, provided the cancer hadn't spread, called the Winkelman B1 Variation. The surgery would remove the leg above the knee, turn it around 180 degrees, disarticulate the hip and put the knee where the hip was, and the knee becomes the new hip with the ankle with the foot still attached, which will function as a knee for the prosthetic. The one catch was that if they went in and found things were worse than the tests showed, the Winkelman would be negated and the whole leg would have to be removed. John went into the operation not knowing if he would come out without any leg or with a partial leg and the promise of a high-functioning prosthetic.

In the meantime John was still coaching at SMCC, and he had to tell the team what was happening.

"That was hard," he said. "It was hard for me. It was hard for them."

John tells of one kid on the tam who was an ex-Marine. He had seen this stuff before. All the kids were shocked. This kid's face was white, so much so that John asked him to stay behind after the rest of the players had left.

"You okay," John asked.

"I've seen legs," he said.

"I know," John said. "I'm going to be all right you know."

"I know," he said. "but still . . ."

That was a tough moment.

Still, John has handled everything with remarkable grace and courage.

"The one thing that came to me, even before the surgery, was the concept that life is relentless," he said. "Life is just going to keep coming."

John added, "I haven't spent a lot of time saying 'Why me?' If anything, somehow I have an ability to handle this. So maybe I handle it better that the next guy. So in that case, "Why not me?"

There have been black moments, but for the most part John has realized he doesn't have a choice. He needs to move forward, to move on.

"The main thing is, it's the things you learn in sports," he said. "You've got four fouls in the second half. You have to figure out how to play, how to stay on the floor. You lose a close game. It's hard. But how do you bounce back?"

John returns to the dunk, a smile on his face. A good small college player, he always worked harder than most and he could always, always jump.

He's smiling because the play, for all its highlight quality, never appeared in a game report or stat sheet, except as a missed shot.

"That's a bit like life," he said. "Some of the best

> stuff never shows up. It doesn't mean it isn't important or doesn't have meaning."
>
> Best shot I ever missed.

I wish I could articulately state what Mike Whaley means to me. He has known me now for over forty-three years. He has seen the best I have to offer as a human being, and he has seen the worst of me too. Yet somehow, he has stayed a remarkable and steadfast friend.

The last comment on "the dunk that never was" belongs to Bill Fitzgerald who was on the court that day and responded to Mike's column by writing to me, "This one brought tears to my eyes. I was 50 feet behind the play. The call was bad, and the hoop should have counted! Just saying."

Building a Leg

In late April Bruce and I started walking outside again. It was over 125 days since the surgery and I was walking using crutches. The red-brick sidewalks in our neighborhood overlooking Casco Bay are beautiful to look at but often uneven, buckled by tree roots and winter frosts, and slick with dew in the early mornings. We made our way through the early morning fog and mists as the sun rose over the bay each day—me with my left pant leg empty and a firm grip on the handles of my crutches. I still needed to be careful not to swing my backward-facing foot too quickly and it must have been the slowest walking Bruce has ever done but it felt so good to be outside and moving. In early May I began the fitting process for my artificial leg

In the second week of May I started the next phase of my recovery.

CaringBridge Post May 7, 2013

Back to the prosthetist and other stuff
139 days after the surgery

It's now Sunday night. Tomorrow I am:

A. Going back to see Keith Cornell, the prosthetist who is building my leg, to try on the socket (the part of the artificial leg that fits onto the existing limb) they have fitted for me. After they made a cast of my leg and foot last week, they used that cast to build a plaster-of-paris model of my foot and leg and spent the week fitting the socket to the model. Tomorrow we will see how it fits on me! After that they will design and attach the artificial ankle and foot to the socket and in two or three more weeks I should have the initial version of my new leg.

B. My niece Laura and her fiancé Brandon have organized a group to move me—and all the crap that goes with me—back upstairs. They are coming tomorrow after work. I have felt strong enough to live upstairs for a week or so and we were just waiting for the right time to move. Well, that time came when we had an offer to rent the apartment I am living in. So upstairs I go. It will be good to be back where I belong. I am going up and down the stairs several times a day and in general, stairs are not an issue. I just go slow, and one hand keeps an iron grip on the railing while I use a crutch with the other.

C. Most importantly, thank you to everyone who continues to reach out to Cindy and me to offer encouragement and support. While complications from the surgery could still occur, I am well on my way to the next phase: learning to walk again. There is still much I cannot do, and I suppose some things I may never do again, but I am planning and working to be able to everything I can do and do it as soon as possible.

D. Cindy has been and continues to be a rock. I wouldn't have made the strides (bad choice of word) I have without her. Her courage, emotional strength, and physical abilities are often hidden beneath her gentle countenance, but she is a fierce and able companion.

As May went on, I continued to make the drive from Portland to Beverly, Massachusetts, to Keith Cornell's office. Over several weeks we kept working on refining the fit and design of my artificial leg. Keith had been referred to me by Nick Helides, a college friend of my brother-in-law Dave. Nick's office was in the same complex as Keith's and we were able to visit a couple of times before and after my appointments. Nick's referral is just one of the small pieces that all came together to make my recovery possible.

When Nick learned of my rotationplasty surgery he had contacted me to tell me of the prosthetist who had built a leg for one of his clients' sons who had a rotationplasty surgery as a young boy. Finding a prosthetist who had experience with rotationplasty prosthetics had been one of the most difficult parts of my journey and Nick's referral, in the end, closed that part of the loop.

Keith's lab had been hard at work refining our prototypes. After weeks of casting, measuring, weighing, and metal and plastic bending, we had a leg and I was able to slip it on, buckle and strap myself in and stand upright. Of course, I couldn't put any weight on the new leg. It still felt great simply to have something below the heel of my left foot after months of nothingness. Our plan was to have the final leg ready when the doctors gave me the final clearance to bear weight.

While Keith was building the leg, I was hard at work with the physical therapists at New England Rehab Hospital–Portland. Anne-Marie, Sophie, and the others at NERHP were the perfect combination of taskmasters and supporters. I was a motivated patient and they worked diligently to increase my range of motion and strength both in my new, shortened left leg and my right leg which was going to take a much larger role than before as I learned to walk again. We stretched muscles and tendons and I used an upper-body ergometer to increase my cardiovascular ability. After months of relative inactivity, I had lost both weight and muscle mass. At my lowest weight after the surgery, I weighed 160 pounds on my six-two frame. I had gone into the surgery at a little over 190 pounds. Even after accounting for the lost weight from the amputation I was many pounds below my fighting weight. At the rehab hospital I worked to get in shape so I could begin to learn to walk again.

I had an X-ray appointment scheduled for June 21. If, as expected, the results confirmed the bone growth we had seen all along I would be cleared to begin to walk on my new leg. I needed to be strong enough to do so.

Adaptation

CaringBridge Post
May 30, 2013
The "end of the beginning"
162 days after the surgery

In 1942, talking about the Allies' response to Germany in WWII, Winston Churchill said, "Now is not the end. It is not even the beginning of the end. But it is, perhaps, the end of the beginning."

That quote captures my present feelings very well. In the last several days, as I move closer and closer to getting my artificial leg, I am realizing more than ever before that I am on a long journey. And, that despite all I have been through to this point I am still in the very early stages of that journey.

I have had a massive, life-changing surgery. I have recovered very well physically, mentally, and emotionally from the surgery. I have been patient in my recovery and diligent in my rehab to get to this point. Tomorrow I will be able to put my new leg on and even though I will be limited in my use of the leg for the next two weeks, I am ending the beginning of this long process and moving to the next part of the journey.

The reality of my life as an amputee is beginning to settle upon me. I am sure of my ability to handle the physical parts of this reality. I will learn to walk. I will return to a normal workday life. I will golf again. Those things will be accomplished by repetition and effort and will.

I am less sure of the emotional parts of this new life. For the past eight months, since before the surgery, I have had the goal of getting a new artificial leg that would allow me to return to a life like I had before. Well, now that the moment has arrived and I realize that, of course, my life will not be like it was before. It can't be.

I will be learning to live in a new reality. One where it takes 30 minutes to get dressed in the morning and a set of stairs, while not insurmountable, still requires forethought and care. Where grabbing my shoes and going for a run on a hot afternoon becomes a process instead of a reaction. It seems obvious to say, and I have known it intellectually for months, but the directness of the different kind of life I will now live is staring me in the face and I know my life will never be the same.

The truth of that sentiment gives me pause.

I know that I will adapt, and I suspect that a year from now I will see this time very differently, but at this moment I am coming to grips with the fact that I have reached my goal of getting a leg and realizing that the goal is not an end, not even the beginning of an end but, as Churchill said, "perhaps the end of the beginning."

CaringBridge Post
June 1, 2013
One small step
164 days after the surgery

I picked up my leg yesterday. That's a unique type of statement, isn't it? Keith Cornell and everyone at Cornell Brothers worked very hard to get the leg ready for me to take home as promised. John, the employee who was responsible for the machining and detail work on the leg, worked especially hard because he had his own surgery scheduled for Wednesday and had promised to complete my leg no matter what before he left. He delivered. I have added a picture of the leg to my photos. The leg consists of a carbon foot with an ankle that rotates 20 degrees in either direction. The foot is designed to return energy to my leg with each stride, just like a human foot. The foot is attached to a socket that holds my own, backward-facing foot and has hinged "knee" braces on either side of my ankle. The knee supports are connected to a sleeve that fits over my thigh (the calf of my rotated leg) and the sleeve is connected to a hinged titanium brace to support my hip (the knee that was fused to my pelvis during my surgery). The brace is to prevent my hip/knee from being stressed and damaged by any type of severe side to side stressors. It's kind of like the brace a running back might wear to protect the ligaments in his knee from the force of a tackle from the side. The whole affair at the hip is held in place by a very soft leather belt just below my waist. I wore the leg home and while it felt good to have it on, the effort to move with it was draining. I can wear the leg but not put much weight on it for the next two weeks. After my June 21 appointment with Dr. Ferrone I will be clear to start full gait training—I will learn to walk with the leg. To paraphrase Neil Armstrong, this is one small step for me (and, uh, not much has changed for mankind). Overall, I am very focused on doing as much as I can with the leg while not doing too much until I get the all clear from Dr. Ferrone.

The Day Before I Was Cleared to Walk

CaringBridge Post
June 21, 2013
Golf with Matt, Travis, and Harry
184 days after the surgery

On the evening of June 19th, I called Matt Richards, the basketball coach and athletic director at Southern Maine Community College. Matt had played college ball in my last year as the head coach at Colby-Sawyer College. The year he played for me he was a dedicated freshman who was backing up a sophomore who was one of the best three-point shooters in the country. As a freshman Jim Durrell had set the all-time, all-division NCAA record for three-point accuracy by making 9 of 9 three-pointers in a game. Matt's job every day in practice was to make Jimmy work hard. In our offense we ran multiple screens on each possession to attempt to free Jimmy for good looks at the hoop. As a result, Matt who was 6 foot tall and weighed 160 pounds soaking wet, was often black-and-blue from 6'5", 220-pound forwards trying to knock him down as we attempted to get Jimmy open. Matt never complained. He took it as a personal challenge to guard the hell out of Jimmy and fight over, under, or through the hundred or more screens he faced every day in practice. When game time came Jimmy was in great shape, used screens very well, and scored because of Matt's effort in practices that nobody outside of our team ever saw. But everyone on the team, especially Jimmy, knew how valuable Matt was to our team.

In the years since, Matt had become a successful college basketball coach in his own right and his teams at SMCC were perennially at the top of their conference and ranked among the best in the country in their division. As an athletic director he worked tirelessly to develop a program that allowed all the athletes at SMCC the best opportunities for success. Part of that hard work, as it is for every college athletic administrator, is raising funds. Matt had started a day of golf and camaraderie to raise money for the athletic department and I had played on his team every year of the event. Our scramble team consisted of Matt and me, Travis Hersom, who also had played for me at Colby-Sawyer, and Harry Fullerton, a longtime friend of mine. We all looked forward to the event each June played on the oceanside course at Prouts Neck in Scarborough, Maine.

This year though, no one—including me—expected me to play. I had been on bed rest since the surgery and had only received my leg two weeks prior. I hadn't even stood up on the new leg without crutches yet. When I called Matt to tell him I wanted to play he asked two questions: "Did Cindy say it was okay?" and "What did the doctors say?" I told him that Cindy was okay with it, if not overjoyed, and that the doctors were too. That last part was a bit of a stretch—the scramble was on June 20th and I had my six-month and last X-ray scheduled for June 21st. After the May X-ray, Dr. Ferrone had said that my femur and my pelvis bones appeared fused but that the protocol was for six months of inactivity and he didn't want to risk any injury or excessive stress on the point where he had screwed the two bones together. I was to come back in June for the final X-ray and okay to begin activity . . . In my opinion I was okay to play golf.

The morning of the event I put on my leg and grabbed my crutches to head to the car. My golf clubs were in the back where they had been since the previous fall. I was nervous as I made the

20-minute drive to the course. When I arrived, Matt had reserved a parking space for me right next to the events tent and the pro shop. I got out and several of Matt's players swarmed my car to grab my clubs and get me situated. It was good catching up with many of the people I saw each year at the event, and I made a few tentative practice swings and rolled a few putts on the practice green. I was walking with my leg on but using my crutches to support most of my weight except when I stood over the ball to swing.

It was a great day. I was tired almost from the beginning but pumped up with adrenaline because I was out playing with my friends. We were playing a scramble, where everyone hits a drive, the team selects the best shot, everyone hits the next shot, and that process is repeated until the ball is in the hole. I was unsteady, weak, and tired, but I managed to score a birdie on my own ball when, on one hole we used my drive, my second shot and I made the birdie putt!

It was a thrill.

The next day, 184 days after the surgery, I made the trip to Boston for X-rays and Dr. Ferrone confirmed what we all had thought. My bones had fused, and I could begin formal gait training. I was going to learn how to walk again! I made an appointment with the physical therapists at New England Rehab Hospital in Portland for the following Monday morning.

After a week of daily work with the physical therapiss that focused on flexibility, strength, and posture, I was walking better but still haltingly. At the end of the first week (186 days after the surgery) I made the decision in conjunction with my therapist Anne-Marie to not use my crutches but to walk only with a cane.

In addition to my work at the hospital I also played a nine-hole round of golf with my buddies in the Construction League—my league for my weekly game for several years. The guys were concerned, probably rightly so, that I was too weak to play. But I explained that I couldn't hurt the rebuilt leg and that all I had to lose was my pride. I told them that if I fell down, I would just get up and try it again. That first nine holes I had two pars and a birdie. It was one more moment that approached normalcy—at least my new normal.

In the meantime, I was struggling with the reality of what my new normal would be. I wrote these thoughts:

"I sometimes awake at night or early in the morning with an anxiety about how weak I may become in my old age. Before I lost my leg, I had always assumed I would be one of the "strong" old men; very fit until the end and then die in my sleep one night. Now, as I come to grips each day with how my life has changed, I am sometimes afraid of facing old age as a disabled man who will need to rely on others. Who will my caregivers be? Cindy will age with me. What if I need to care for her? What if my caregivers ignore me or don't respond to my calls or pleas? What happens if I am ever too weak to use my artificial leg or my crutches or even a walker? If I need help for the basic daily activities?

"Before losing my leg I never dealt with these fears. Now they visit regularly."

Closing CaringBridge

CaringBridge Post
August 2, 2013
The last post
228 days after the surgery

On Monday August 5th I celebrated my 54th birthday. On Saturday and Sunday, I played in the Riverside Golf Association Member/Guest Tournament. My partner, Jeremy, and I shot an 87 on Saturday and I shot a 93 on Sunday—not winning scores but we had fun and, more importantly, I was out on two legs chasing a golf ball.

In the months and days that have passed since my surgery on December 20th I have been blessed with supportive family and friends who have seen me through an incredible emotional and, at times, tough physical journey.

When I received the okay to begin to bear weight on my artificial leg in late June, I began to work towards accomplishing the two physical goals I had carried into my amputation surgery. First and foremost, in November of 2012 when we decided that the amputation was the best course of action, I had promised my niece Susan that I would dance with her on her wedding day (July 20th). The week before her wedding I asked my physical therapist to dance with me a bit to see if I had the balance and strength to fulfill that promise. We danced, in the workout gym, with no music, so I could be sure I was able to dance. The dance with Susan the afternoon of her beautiful wedding meant more than I can say. Secondly, I had set the goal that I would play July 6th and 7th in the St. Peter's Golf Tournament with my longtime team of Peter, Harry, and Bob. I did, although the heat and my lack of conditioning left me exhausted after the Saturday round. I came home Saturday evening, took off my leg, grabbed a pillow, and slept for two hours on the living room floor. On Sunday morning I felt refreshed and ready, and we went out as a team and shot a round of 61 in the scramble. Pretty Respectable.

On August 20 it will have been eight months since I laid down on the gurney to undergo the operation that would save my life and change it forever. While I went into the surgery hopeful of a good outcome and expecting the best, I never could have imagined how the next months would ultimately unfold. As those of you who have followed these posts and supported me through these months know, I experienced a huge range of emotions and uncovered parts of myself that had been buried too long. The joy I have in the mornings as I wake and watch the rising sun slowly light up the city, spreading from the far-off horizon to my back deck as it rises higher in the sky, cannot be measured. I appreciate life and most importantly, the people in my life, with a depth and a clarity that I did not have in December. I am not only very glad to be alive, but I am also glad to be alive with one leg. It is who I am, and I continue to live by the equation **Life > Limb**.

My family, especially my lovely wife, Cindy, along with my mother and my sister were heroic in their efforts to support me. I was not always easy to help and yet they were patient with me. In January I wrote of being "surrounded by angels, by beings with a greater closeness to the power of the universe than I know." In retrospect, if anything, those words are truer today than they were then. I have been blessed spiritually, emotionally, and physically by those in my life.

Our friends have been, and continue to be, amazing: Steve and Deb Jordan for all their support and Steve's tireless work both pre- and post-surgery; Steve White for meeting me in Boston (we'll see each other this Friday) on my trips to Dana Farber; Bill Fitzgerald for deciding that even if he couldn't call me, that he could (and did) decide to respond to every post I wrote with an uplifting comment; Bob, Tony, Jenn, Christine, and others who brought me lunch when I was house-bound; Drew and Paul who drove to Boston; Peg and Paul for the picnics in our kitchen and Tom and the guys for the videos of the mid-winter bonfires; Bruce (for our morning coffee and weightlifting) and Alice for our pizza nights as we continue to make our way through the OTTO's menu; all of my buddies in the golf league who lift me up with their humor (including Eric Theriault, who after I complained about his sarcastic impatience with my walking speed by pointing out that "Hey, I only have one leg," responded, "You've got a leg and a half. Quit complaining!"; Mike Whaley for his tremendous column that captured that lost moment in time on a basketball court years ago; to my business partner and dear friend Eric, who kept our business going and our clients well satisfied through a very tough fall and spring. And there are others, too many to list, who have reached out to me and touched my life in ways that I can never repay except to promise that I will look for ways to help others as I have been helped.

It is the right time to close this post as I can now walk (slowly) without a cane and am focusing on strengthening and stretching my entire body to make the most out of the second chance I have been given. My life has changed. Physically it is obvious that I will never be the same. But different isn't necessarily bad.

Emotionally, I hope to make it obvious that I am not the same person who was wheeled into that operating room 230 days ago. My task is to live my life so that everyone can see what all of you have taught me—that the love of family and friends can overcome any obstacle and teach all of us how to live with clarity and purpose; that setbacks are opportunities to learn and change and grow; that life is greater than limb.

"Cut the Other One Off and Go Pro"

"Golf is the closest game to the game we call life. You get bad breaks from good shots; you get good breaks from bad shots—but you have to play the ball where it lies."

—Bobby Jones

Bobby Jones is arguably the greatest golfer the world has ever seen. He never became a professional golfer even after winning all the major tournaments around the world and competing successfully against the world's best professionals. He retired from competitive golf at twenty-eight and went on to a long career as a lawyer, co-founder of Augusta National Golf Club, and a golf equipment designer. In 1948 he was diagnosed with syringomyelia, a generic term referring to a disorder in which a cyst or cavity forms within the spinal cord. This cyst can expand and elongate over time, destroying the spinal cord and often causing great pain. He died in 1971.

Bobby Jones knew the highest highs. He was feted with

ticker-tape parades in New York. And the lowest lows as his once-strong body failed him and he was confined to a wheelchair. He knew about playing the ball where it lies.

One of the unique things about golf is that each golfer maintains his score and the score of his opponent and calls penalties on himself should they occur. There is no referee calling fouls or an umpire deciding whether a player is safe or not. The score is added up and if there is an infraction, if the balls moves inadvertently or the player grounds his club in a sand trap, the player informs his playing partners of the mistake and adds the penalty to his score for the hole.

As Jones says, the game of golf is not fair or equitable. Sometimes good shots result in bad breaks and other times a bad shot can ricochet off a tee into the middle of a fairway. The golfer's job is to find his ball and plan his next shot. He can't waste time worrying about how the ball got there or whether the break is good or bad—it is what it is.

The parallels to life are obvious but whereas golf is a game where unscrupulous people can cheat (and some do), life can't be cheated. You can try to change the outcome, you can try denying the result, but in the end, it always is what it is. The quicker we figure out how to plan and execute our next step the quicker we move toward whatever the resolution is.

When the ball lands in a bad spot playing golf, a good golfer carefully analyzes his options, determines the risk/reward of the potential next shots, weighs that against his skill set, the match at hand, and the probability of success—chooses an option and executes. Sometimes—oftentimes actually—when faced with a bad lie, the best choice is to make a simple shot to recover back to the middle of the fairway versus trying to hit a courageous shot with a low probability of pulling it off. It is not the sexy or glamorous thing to do but it keeps one from compounding the first mistake into another bad situation.

In life the simpler answer is often the best. It is getting up in the morning and doing what needs to be done—taking care of yourself and the people around you as well as you can each day. It is facing your responsibilities directly and not trying to make the great play but simply recovering from your bad lie to have a good shot the next time. Simple doesn't mean easy. There is a big difference between simple and easy. But most often simple is best and determining what is next by finding the simple solution allows one to make good choices that lead to other good choices.

When I was faced with my cancer diagnosis, surgeries, radiation, and more surgeries I was sure that life wasn't fair. But I never expected it to be. For some reason I was given the ability to quickly accept what was and focus on what was coming next. I never questioned why. And, as I told my friend Mike Whaley when he interviewed me for his column, "If I can handle this better than the next guy, why not me?"

Play it as it lies.

The rarest occurrence in golf is a hole in one. Most amateurs never experience the thrill of a shot hit from the tee arching through the air to land on the green and roll into the cup. There are touring pros who play at the highest level who haven't scored a hole in one, although there are others who have had more than ten. But for us regular folks it remains elusive at best.

In September of 2013, eight months after my amputation, my friend, Gerry Vicenzi, asked me to join him along with Mike Sosnowski and Mike Hachey in a foursome to play a charity event to benefit the Opportunity Alliance, a nonprofit that does tremendous work in the greater Portland area. I had been on my new leg for almost three months by this point and had played maybe eight or ten rounds of golf with varying degrees of success.

That Monday dawned a little bit cold—as September days can be in Maine—and windy. But I was excited to join my group as we played The Woodlands, one of the finest, if not the best, courses in Maine. The Woodlands is now my home course but in September of 2013 it was a treat to play the private course.

Gerry and Mike Hachey were casual golfers who hit more good shots than bad that day. Mike Sosnowski was a solid contributor to our team's success with his steady game. I, on the other hand, vacillated between shots that were eerily reminiscent of my pre-amputation swing and others that looked a lot like a guy playing with a brand-new leg. We knew early in the round that we weren't going to challenge anyone with winning the event and settled into a relaxing and enjoyable rhythm for the round.

When we reached the seventeenth hole, a long par-three playing about 185 yards to a downhill green with water on two sides, the wind was directly in our faces. In golfing parlance, it was a "three-club" wind—it was blowing hard!

At the tee there was a sign announcing that the prize for a hole in one was a $10,000 beach vacation. I joked with the young lady who was the spotter for the hole (she would ascertain if anyone did in fact make a hole in one to win the prize) that my days of running on the beach were behind me and that with this wind we would be lucky to reach the green. She said that very few people had even got close to the green let alone the flag.

When it was my turn to hit, I chose a 3Hybrid, a club I hit about 200 yards. I thought that with the downhill to the green and the wind in my face that a well-struck shot might find the front of the green. I wasn't hoping for anything more.

As I stood over the ball waiting to strike it, the wind gusts seemed to pick up. I waited for a break in the wind and swung. I made perfect contact with the center of the clubface and the ball started toward the green with a slight draw, low into the wind. As it flew, we could tell it was on a good line, moving a bit from right to left toward the flag stick. The ball landed at the front of the green, bounced, and then rolled about fifiteen feet right into the cup!

No one was more surprised than me, but I think Mike Sosnowski was the happiest of all of us. He was like a kid on Christmas morning as he hopped around! I was hopping around too—as much as I could on one leg.

The strange thing was while I was excited to watch the ball roll into the hole, I was also somewhat still inside. The shot was good, the result lucky, but the moment was sublime. While I smiled and hugged my playing companions I was struck even more by the uniqueness of my situation. My leg was gone and my reality somehow confirmed by this so rare of golfing events.

It was a wonderful moment that makes me smile when I reflect on it, even today. My good friend Tony Mancini called me when he heard about the shot. As I answered my phone, he didn't even introduce himself or say hello. He simply said, "Cut the other one off and go pro!" I nearly dropped the phone I was laughing so hard.

The Last Chapter

My story is long and complicated. I have had highs and lows and I continue to feel those highs and lows to this day eight years after they took my leg. I wish I could report a "happily ever after" ending, but life is not that easy, pretty, or simple. As I have found out first-hand, life is a messy, slog-through affair. That said, I wouldn't trade my life for anyone's. I am content and that is so much more than most people ever achieve.

I continue to focus on the things I can do much more than the things I can't. One of the areas I can focus on is improving my golf game. Golf is one of the few areas where I can still compete. With the help of Paul Piveronis and Casey Cox, two PGA Professionals at my club, I have rebuilt a swing that allows me to compete at a high level. I have lowered my handicap to single digits and generally score well in regional and national amputee and disabled golfer tournaments.

I take a great deal of pleasure out of playing with able-bodied golfers who don't know me and initially reflect that subtle "Oh no" when they see a guy with a prosthetic approach the first tee.

After I match or outdrive them on the first tee and generally hit shots they can't, their attitude starts to change. When I finish the round with a score that is as good as—or perhaps better than—theirs, they often tell me how special it was to play a round with me. Maybe in some small way I can help people in general realize that we all have things we need to overcome—some of us are just more obvious with our disability. But the rest of us still need to see that no one is really whole. Emotional issues, physical issues, and cognitive impairments—they are all part of the human condition and each of us has an inherent value that needs to be recognized.

One of the things I did after losing my leg was to help establish the Amputee Association of Maine (AAM), a 501(c)3 nonprofit. I, and several others, realized that the path of an amputee hadn't changed too much even as advances in medicine and amputee outcomes had greatly improved. Once it becomes medically necessary to amputate someone's leg or arm, the pathway was still rooted in a medical model rather than recognizing the whole person whose life was about to change forever. The surgeon often tells the patient something along the lines of "We need to take your leg. After surgery you will be with us in the hospital for several days and then we will send you to a rehab hospital where they will work with you to make sure you are safe to go home alone. At some point post-surgery, you will need to pick a prosthetist to build your artificial leg—several of them will come into your room to speak with you. Choose one and you'll be on your way. Good luck."

The reality is obviously much more nuanced. The Amputee Association of Maine has built a website to allow amputees, their families, and the professionals that serve them access to resources to help in all aspects of the life of an amputee.

The AAM also began the Maine Amputee Open, a thirty-six-hole golf tournament for amputees and able-bodied golfers. The two-day event is played for one overall champion and amputee and able-bodied first, second, and third place finishers. We have had the great fortune of Gorham Savings Bank serving as our naming sponsor since we started the event. The Maine Amputee Open is part of four days of golf that starts on a Sunday afternoon with an Adapted Golf Clinic, open to anyone with a disability who wants to improve their golf game. Over the years we have worked with amputees and people living with stroke results, brain injuries, and other situations. We have worked with combat-injured vets and helped teach occupational therapists and physical therapists how golf can help in rehab overall. The three hours spent in the Adapted Golf Clinic on Sunday is my favorite time at our events.

We also sponsor a classic corporate scramble on Monday afternoon to raise money for the AAM and allow our out-of-state amputee golfers a chance to see the course before playing in the Maine Amputee Open. We are fortunate that we have had some of the top amputee golfers from around the country play in our event.

It was at the First Gorham Savings Bank Maine Amputee Open that I had the seminal moment since losing my leg. I was being interviewed at the golf tournament by a local TV sports reporter. The young reporter probably wasn't older than twenty-five when she asked me, "Do you ever wish you had your leg back?"

I swallowed, thought a moment, and replied, "Of course I do. But, if I had to give up everything I have learned about myself in order to get my leg back, then no. It wouldn't be a fair trade."

Author's Note:

There are many people mentioned in this book. People who helped me or Cindy in ways big and small; people who found that helping someone in need was good for their souls too. We are lucky to have the friends and family we have.

There are many other people whose story could not be woven into my memoir but who played big parts in helping me come out the other side of losing my leg. I know I can't possibly remember everyone and that I run the risk of forgetting someone. To that person(s) I apologize in advance.

People like:

I have mentioned my business partner Eric Anton previously. But I need to say that Eric is much more than a business partner. He is like a brother to me and his personal support and professional competence allowed me to convalesce without worry. After I wrote this book, he graciously agreed to edit the content for grammar. Like all parts of our relationship, his efforts made me look good.

Alice Shea who not only put in long hours as we prepped the downstairs apartment for my return after surgery, but who also gave her husband Bruce Davis permission to hang out with me and work out and have our talks (that continue to this day) three or more mornings each week. Alice was committed to helping the four of us try valiantly to make our way through the entire OTTO's pizza menu while I was confined to my apartment after my surgery.

Peg and Paul who in addition to making sure my business kept functioning and driving us to Boston early after my surgery for Doctor's appointments, also brought picnic lunches for us to enjoy indoors in a Maine winter.

Bob Danielson who walked up from his law office in downtown Portland in a snowstorm to have lunch with me.

Tony Mancini who checked often on me, Cindy, and my mother to make sure we were all okay.

Deb Jordan's support of me and equally important, her support of Cindy, can't be overstated.

Brian Huey. He showed up with his daughters on the way home after a dance gig and brought some much-needed levity into a cold winter's day.

Willie Audet who called often to check on me and Cindy.

My brothers Michael and Patrick. We share the same backstory in a lot of ways, and we certainly share the same off-kilter, maybe a little sick, sense of humor. They cracked me up with things that were probably funny only to us.

Mark and Sue Hilton who let me know in no uncertain terms what I meant to them and allowed me to become part of their family.

My great friends in the Construction League—the oldest golf league (more than fifty years old) in the US not affiliated with a golf course or country club. Their brand of support and humor saw me through many dark days and provided impetus to get out and play as soon as I was able.

The BFAH Golf Society. Decorum prevents me from saying too much. But to have been voted BFAH of the Year while laid up in bed and unable to attend our annual Cape Cod trip, was one of the nicest things anybody did for me in my bed-rest recovery.

All the people associated with the SMCC athletic program who reached out to me—players and coaches who let me know I was missed and appreciated.

Ann-Marie (and Shelly) and the outstanding staff at New England Rehab Hospital who took my drive and determination and channeled it into meaningful exercise and activity to get me up and walking on my prosthetic quickly and safely.

My former players at Keene State College and Colby-Sawyer College who called and wrote letters. The chance to have coached you was (and remains) one of my greatest privileges. As well as the coaches who succeeded me at KSC and C-SC who both reached out with good wishes.

Several of my clients who wrote the nicest things on the Caring Bridge pages. I have had the privilege of helping you professionally and am fortunate to have experienced your caring personally.

The doctors who work so hard to fight back against the illness life throws at their patients. My surgeons were amazing and especially Dr. Carl Schuler our longtime family doctor for his house calls during my rehab.

About the Author

John LeMieux was born in Milwaukee, Wisconsin, before moving to Maine at age one. There is family speculation that his fear of small spaces started with his first basinet—a dresser drawer which may have been closed when he cried.

He was a college basketball coach for nine years after earning a bachelor's degree from Lyndon State College in Vermont and a master's degree from Indiana University in Bloomington, Indiana. His women's basketball teams at Keene State College won back-to-back Division II ECAC championships while setting school records for wins in each of his two seasons at KSC. After KSC he initiated the men's basketball program at Colby-Sawyer College, leading his first team to a 13–12 record against Division III varsity opponents.

After leaving coaching John began to work in financial services with Merrill Lynch and other firms before co-founding Anton LeMieux Financial Group with his partner Eric Anton in 2009. The business now serves clients across the nation with offices in Falmouth, Maine, and Naples and Daytona Beach, Florida.

John lives in Portland, Maine, with his wife Cindy and enjoys competitive golf, playing in amputee and other tournaments throughout the eastern United States.

Made in the USA
Las Vegas, NV
12 December 2022

62063187R00142